William Rickenbacker's
Savings and Investment Guide

By the same author

WOODEN NICKELS
DEATH OF THE DOLLAR
THE FOURTH HOUSE
FROM FATHER TO SON
THE TWELVE-YEAR SENTENCE

William Rickenbacker's Savings and Investment Guide

WILLIAM F. RICKENBACKER

David McKay Company, Inc.

NEW YORK

Library of Congress Cataloging in Publication Data

Rickenbacker, William F   1928-
William Rickenbacker's Savings and investment guide.

Bibliography: p.
Includes index.—
1. Investments—Dictionaries. 2. Finance, Personal
—Dictionaries. I. Title.
HG 4513.R52   1976—   332'.024   76-4984
ISBN 0-679-50596-2

For Carroll

UXORI   MEAE

UXORI MEAE

AMORE PECUNIAQUE SAPIENTISSIMAE

QUAE MAGNA DILIGENTIA MIHI DILIGENTIAM DEDIT

Contents

William Rickenbacker's
Savings and Investment Guide

How to Use This Book

About a hundred books a year are published under some such title as *How to Get Rich,* or *How to Avoid Catastrophe,* or *How to Manage Your Investments,* or *How to Cope with Inflation.* They're a dreary lot.

They fall into two groups. One group is so full of technical jargon that average people find themselves up the creek without a paddle. "This is beyond me," they say. The other group is so simplified that it doesn't really help. It addresses the kindergarten and deals with trivia, giving no insight into the workings of a system that uses money and investments.

Until now there has been no book that I know of that has been written for the average person and has also included the lessons and policies (wisdom, if you wish) that a long career in the investment business can furnish.

There are reasons for this failure in the past. The average person wasn't ever faced with such difficult conditions before. One could, until recently, run his personal affairs quite successfully by working steadily, saving regularly, putting the savings into some combination of blue-chip stocks, long-term bonds and savings accounts, and weathering the occasional storms that are the therapeutic restoratives of an economy based on freedom of action.

Now all of that is under suspicion. When gigantic concerns like Penn Central, Lockheed, Franklin National, W.T. Grant, Equity Funding, and the real estate trusts have gone broke or are tottering on the edge of collapse, who's to say that any old blue-chip corporation is automatically a sound long-term investment?

When the holders of municipal bonds find themselves facing severe capital losses because the credit rating of city after city is going downhill, who's to say a man is wise to buy bonds?

When the buying power of the currency is rotting away, each year, by 10 percent or more, what's so good about savings accounts yielding 5 percent, or even long-term bonds yielding 7 or 8 percent?

The disorder that is the result of many years of political mismanagement has now driven far enough into the fabric of our society to affect the financial planning of the average family. The average family was always subject to swings in the economy—unemployment and reduced paychecks were the usual results. But you could prepare for those shocks by laying some cash aside, and it used to be that your cash reserves actually *gained* in buying power during hard times, because the price level in general tended to come down.

Not so any longer! Now you have the worst of both worlds. The economy staggers along, with high rates of unemployment, and yet you find your cash reserves losing their buying power even when you've relied on them to tide you over any period of layoffs or reduced earnings.

For the first time in your life, perhaps, you realize that your *financial* planning (the way you handle your savings) is just as important as your *economic* planning (the way you set aside some income and add it to your savings).

Thus for the first time the average person is in need of something that will go beyond the ABC level of describing what a savings account is, and explains just why savings accounts are no longer the automatic shelters for average families, what proportion of wealth should be in them nevertheless, and how to handle the funds removed from savings accounts for better deployment elsewhere.

The great C.S. Lewis used to say that a man who couldn't

explain Christianity in the language of the street either didn't understand it or didn't believe in it. I think the same is true of investment planning. This book is an attempt to discuss finances and investments in everyday language but without diluting the seriousness of the issues.

The layout of the book reflects these aims. It is arranged in alphabetical order, so you can find what you need in a hurry. But what I have put into the individual essays and entries has not been watered down. I have described many traps and pitfalls to avoid; and have told how you can spot them before they get too close for comfort. I have given the results of my own long-term study—boiled down into simple "rules" such as, "keep your eye on the cash" (a rule ignored by the financial analysts of Penn Central before the crisis). Some of the rules I have learned are so basic that they could easily be dismissed as mere peasant-wisdom. But I have also observed that the peasants have survived for thousands of years.

The book isn't intended for sit-down, straight-through reading, although it could probably be approached that way. Use it, instead, for reference and consultation as you work your way into a newly constructed approach to your own financial planning.

How long will this age last? If it were a matter of a season, something subject to change with the next election, this book would perhaps be gray-bearded and feeble before it could make its way into the bookstores. But our troubles— your troubles—are the children of a half century of abuse, and these wrongs won't be righted overnight. Inflation has become the model and the standard of government, and this is the case throughout the world. Deficit budgets and enormous borrowings are the order of the day, and this also holds true throughout the world. The results have percolated throughout society. State and local governments no longer see why they have to be the only ones to balance their budgets. Corporations report profits that might be turned into deficits if the effects of inflation were fully reflected in the accounts. Investors who spend the entirety of their cash dividends may be living in a fool's paradise. Employees grow restless when they discover that their wage increases hardly begin to offset the damage done by inflation. Careful men, planning for their retirement, find the fruits of years of patient saving withered away in the plague-winds of inflated currency.

The results of this situation and its interconnections are now so widespread that you could speak of monetary disorder as an "institution" in our society. "The Establishment" *is* the problem. And that is why it is so evident that we'll have this problem with us for a long time to come. It is a great mistake to foresee some financial Armageddon—things just don't happen that way. Error simply becomes more institutionalized than before, and confusion becomes more acceptable and more understandable, "because that's the way it is." There is a desperate inertia concerning these matters. Meanwhile, you must study to preserve your financial assets through the disorderly times we face.

I foresee inflation continuing and accelerating gradually over the years. We have already reached the point where a constant rate of inflation does nothing to stimulate the economy. This kind of inflation can go on for years. In the absence of any drastic change in our relations with Moscow, I would expect our inflation rate to reach 15 percent by 1980, 50 to 100 percent by 1990, and crisis proportions by the year 2000. A "crisis" occurs when the people no longer use money as a store of value, and refuse to accept it as payment. Naturally an economy that has been running on money is crippled when the money ceases to function. For a period during the crisis, goods and products are withheld from the market; a rudimentary form of exchange appears in barter markets; legal contracts by the millions are torn up; creditors are wiped out; banks collapse; governments issue decrees that are ignored; and there is the danger of civil war.

Investment policy in the years leading up to that eventual "moment of truth" must rest on a deep understanding of the processes at work and of the time scale on which those processes work themselves out. *The Crash That Is Soon Coming* is the title of book after book published in the last twenty years, and we'll see such titles again and again in the next thirty years or so. But that note of shrillness and urgency is out of place—we are engaged with long-term forces and with shorter-term swings in public awareness of those forces. While the currency continues to rot, we'll have bull markets and bear markets in stocks, bonds, interest rates, precious metals, commodities, coins and Swiss francs. It will become more and more painfully evident that to maneuver is to survive. No one single perception will always do; no one single policy will work throughout.

I wish it were not so. But it *is* so, and you cannot hope to survive financially unless you see the situation with clear eyes. The quack and the charlatan will always promise to show you how to make a fortune. The lessons of experience and research which you will find in these pages are sure to preserve you from grievous error. And learning how to hang on to your assets is the first requirement in learning how to show a profit on them.

Good luck to you, and may you be filled with the virtues of the successful investor: intelligence, patience, and courage.

W.F.R.

Savings and Investment Guide

A

account executive
  See **broker**.

accounting
You should design an accounting system that shows your financial arrangements from two different angles. One view—the **balance sheet**—shows the static condition as of one moment in time: what you own (what it's all worth), what you owe, and how much is left over (your equity). The other view—the income statement—shows the *flow* of payments during a period of time: receipts, expenditures, and the difference between the two (profit or loss).

accrual vs. cash
Your accounting system will probably be adequate if you record every transaction that involves the payment or receipt of cash. That's the "cash basis" accounting system. A more subtle system, the "accrual basis," strives to report the income and expenses as if they occurred smoothly over a period of time rather than in lumps. Thus, if you expect to

receive a large lump payment for work done over many years, a cash-basis account will show that payment received all at once, while an accrual-basis account will show some portion of the receipt "accrued" in each of the years it is related to. Most corporate accounts are on the accrual basis. Most personal accounts are on the cash basis. Even when accruals are used, the cash remains the important thing. Keep your eye on the cash!

accrued interest
Most bonds pay interest twice a year. As the payment date nears, the amount of interest to be paid is gradually added to the market price of the bond as the interest accrues. On the date of payment the market price drops by the amount of the accrued interest payment. When you buy a bond, there will be a separate statement of the amount of accrued interest. Then, even though you have bought the bond only the day before, if you receive the semi-annual interest payment the next day, you get a full six months of interest. In effect, by adding the accrued interest to your cost, you "paid" the former holder just less than six months' interest.

advance-decline line
A "technical" tool that measures the ratio between the number of stocks that went up in a given period and the number that went down. I find it useful only at major tops and bottoms, once every five years or so.

advice
There's no shortage of advice in the investment world. (See the appendices, which list various publications and other sources of investment advice and information.) But, after you've lined up a few sources of steady supply, what do you do with the information? How should you *use* the advice? A few general rules: 1) don't consider the advice to be sacred or infallible; 2) don't think you have to act immediately; 3)

don't try to find the "average" opinion; 4) don't become addicted to a single source or a single "system." Investigate several sources that seem to be about your speed. Watch them for a while to see if they are consistent, if they make simple common sense, if they write so you can understand them or with the objective of confusing you and making you think they're members of a secret society. A good test: Send them a letter asking a serious question (Should I buy an annuity? What about Mexican gold coins?), and see how they treat you. If they ignore you, ignore them. If they come back with red-hot opinions without bothering to ask you if you're young or old, rich or poor, healthy or sick, forget them. If they ask for more money, forget them. If they reply quickly and politely, asking for enough information about you to make a reasonable recommendation, stick with them; they're trying to do a professional job. But you should still move cautiously. Don't commit everything to one situation or to one type of advice. It may take two years for you to find out whether the advice has been good, average, or bad. Watch out especially for the sign of the quack: the guy who issues a two-faced opinion ("It may be a long while before the stock goes up, but we think it's a winner") and then, in a later issue, pretends that he was right all along—which he can do no matter what happens to the stock. (If it goes down, he reminds you he said, "It may be a long while before the stock goes up"; if it goes up, he reminds you that he said, "we think it's a winner.") Old saying: "Free advice is worth exactly what you paid for it."

advisory services
Here are the main sources of investment advice, with a few general comments about each. For specific details and evaluations of the major operations, see the appendix.

banks

The larger banks have investment-advisory operations. They all charge a minimum fee that makes it impractical for anyone with less than $200,000 or so to use their services. The expense would be tolerable if the service were useful, but there is hardly a bank in the country that does better than the stock market averages. There are three main reasons why banks are lousy investors: 1) they are set up to concentrate on lending, not owning; 2) the larger banks make their profits on corporate deposits, and are naturally uninterested in committing suicide by saying something nasty about the stock of *any* corporation that might open an account with them; and 3) the banks are tightly regulated, and every regulated industry takes on the attitudes and habits of the regulators, the bureaucrats who would rather "look good" by avoiding mistakes than "stick their neck out" by doing something imaginative or something new. Forget banks. They're slow death.

brokers

Most brokerage houses maintain research departments whose job is to discover and publicize new investment opportunities. If the broker is an underwriter, beware: in case of conflict, the broker will always issue optimistic evaluations of companies it has an underwriting connection with. If the broker isn't an underwriter, still beware: it has a greater interest in issuing "buy" recommendations than "sell" recommendations, simply because almost all of its customers might be tempted to buy, but only those who own a specific stock would be in a position to sell it. The broker makes his money by taking a commission on your purchases and sales of securities; if he can't make a trade, he starves. Therefore his interest is not lined up with your interest, because most of the time an investor does best by buying well and holding long. Individual "account executives" very often redeem the reputation of the brokerage fraternity. The best all-round advice is to select a decent man at a large brokerage firm, preferably on the basis of the personal recommendation of a friend. Then instruct your broker never to bother you with investment advice, and arrange to get your advice from other sources.

hot tips

In twenty years of active investment management, I have heard dozens of genuine hot tips from authoritative sources, people in the know, insiders, wise guys, and scoundrels. Almost all of them have been wrong. Luckily I rejected these nuggets of special information and so spared myself the embarrassment of going broke. Don't act on a tip unless it refers to a company you would like to invest in anyway.

letters

"Investment letters" or "market letters" are a highly specialized branch of the publishing business. There are about four hundred different "letters." The average one has fewer than one thousand subscribers. The biggest is probably Standard & Poor's *Outlook*, which has about forty-five thousand subscribers. Very few investment letters make a profit on their own. Most of them make their profits from other sources—ads, rental of lists of names of former subscribers, and individual portfolio management. The *Wall Street Journal* refuses to accept their ads, which you will find mainly in *Barron's*. Most letters are priced high, about $100 a year. Avoid those that advertise the end of the world. Before sending them your money, try a refundable short-term trial subscription, and ask for one or two years' worth of back issues.

pals

You can lose your friends by giving them advice that doesn't work out. My father always said he'd rather have the friends than the money, and I agree. Besides, if it does actually work out, they won't be grateful; instead, they'll take the credit themselves for being such financial wizards. So giving free advice to your pals is all risk and no reward. Don't do it. As for accepting their advice free, just remember that it's worth zero. Be polite, thank them, and change the subject. If their advice was really worth something, they'd be selling it for a fee.

portfolio managers

Strictly speaking, a portfolio manager doesn't make it a steady habit to give advice. He engages in running his clients' investment portfolio. However, you can often give a portion of your assets to a portfolio manager and let him handle them, while you retain another portion for your own investment operations, perhaps in an attempt to outshine the professionals with your daring and genius. In such a case, the portfolio manager will usually be happy to give you advice on stocks you may want to put in your "outside" portfolio. But remember: he's not in business to make you look good, is he? Unless he's unusually ethical, he'll squirm a bit from the bad position you've put him in.

trust companies

As a group the trust companies don't invest any better than the trust departments of commercial banks. There may be exceptions. I have heard high praise for the trust investment department of one firm but have no personal knowledge of it. Here also, the minimum fee makes it impractical to join up unless there are a couple of hundred thousand dollars involved. Most trust companies will have a common "pooled" trust whose investment results can be made public. You should measure those results before committing yourself to any given company. Even then, the decision to go to a trust company should be made only when all else fails.

against the box
See **short**. When you sell short while holding an already established position, you're selling short against the box. In effect that's a hedge. No matter which way the stock goes, you break even, losing on one position and gaining on the other. It's a simple way to freeze a profit until later.

agent vs. principal
See **principal**.

alternative investment cost
In figuring the cost of any investment, it's normal to figure what you might have made if you had done something else in the same general field. For instance, if you want to hold a certain amount in cash, you might have to choose between holding currency and opening a savings account. (See **cash**.) If you decide to hold currency, the "alternative investment cost" would be the interest income you gave up by not opening up a savings account. Also called "opportunity foregone," "opportunity cost," "interest foregone," and so on.

American Depositary Receipt (ADR)
Foreign companies' shares are generally not traded directly in this country. Instead, a foreign bank will hold a block of stock in the foreign companies. An American bank will have the authority to issue "warehouse receipts" against the stock held overseas. The warehouse receipts are ADRs. The American bank collects the dividends remitted from the foreign companies, withholds 15 percent tax, pays the tax to Washington, and sends the ADR holder the remainder of

the cash dividend, minus a small fee for handling (about a half-cent per share). It's important to remember that you get a tax credit (i.e., a reduction of tax) on your Form 1040 for the amount of tax withheld by the bank.

amortization
An expense incurred now whose benefits may be spread over many years (amortized) rather than charged against the income of any one year. A write-off. See also **accrual** and **write-off**.

annual reports
Each company issues an annual report to its shareholders, telling them what was done in the last year, giving the accounts (balance sheet and income statement), and looking ahead. The reports can be informative. Avoid companies whose reports are too slick. Before investing in a company, write to its headquarters and ask for the last few annual reports. Compare the achievements with the promises made in earlier years. Get a feel for the "hot-air ratio" in management.

anticipation
To anticipate is not only to foresee but also to make preparations. We all do it. A girl takes a quick look in the mirror before she goes out on a date. The head of an aircraft manufacturing company starts tooling up now for a jet fighter that won't be rolling off the line for several years yet. Anticipation is found wherever you find intelligence functioning, but you never find anticipation so concentrated as it is in the financial markets. And there is a remarkable fact about financial anticipation: it is almost always right. A couple of years before Computer Applications went broke, the stock started sagging. It had been as high as 40. It dropped to 20. A year later it was down to 5 or 4. It dropped, finally, to zero, and the company went out of

business. It is extremely rare to see a stock rising while the company is hitting the skids, or to see a stock droop while the company is blooming. Why should this be? I think it's because there is always a small group of people who actually know what's going to happen to a company, and they aren't necessarily the top men. The shipping clerks, bookkeepers, personnel managers, and suppliers are among the first to recognize a dramatic shift in the company's prospects. Their knowledge spreads among friends and casual acquaintances until it becomes the strongest single factor in the market's evaluation of the stock. Of course there will be competing factions—those who think the company is doing very well, moderately well, average, poorly, very poorly—but the also-rans are always at odds with each other as well as being wrong to boot. They don't gain strength, whereas the true prospects become ever more apparent as time goes on. So major new trends in a company's life are almost always correctly foreseen in a gradual anticipatory movement in the price of the stock. This rule has consequences for you as an investor. You should never think you have such special information that you can disagree with the market price of the stock. Don't argue with the tape! And once the "news" has been made public, don't expect the stock to act in simple harmony with it. The stock is more likely to act in counterpoint. If the stock has anticipated the good news for a couple of years, then there is no *new* reason for the stock to go up when the good news is finally announced. Instead, a lot of those whose interest in the stock was tied exclusively to that one piece of news will now sell and take their profits. Don't buy stocks on the basis of the day's headlines. Those headlines, correctly foreseen a couple of years earlier, have already had their effect on the price of the stock. Hence the proverbial wisdom: Sell on the good news, buy on the bad!

antiques
Not recommended as investments unless you're a specialist. Performance no better than average; negative yield (you pay to store and maintain the "investment"); and difficulty of disposing of the goods at a decent price in hard times.

appreciation
This doesn't mean a vote of thanks for services rendered. In financial talk, it means a rise in price, especially of something held for investment purposes. If you buy at 40 and notice, later, that the market price of your holding is 45, then you have a capital appreciation of 5 points. If the general price level has gone up by the same ratio in the same time, then your appreciation is not "real"—only "nominal" (in name only). If you don't sell your holding, then your appreciation is unrealized. Normally you don't pay taxes on capital appreciation (capital gains) unless and until they've been realized. The tax gatherer keeps his eye on the cash. You should, too.

arbitrage
Trading in two different markets at once, to take advantage of price differentials. You might buy wheat at $3.70 in Chicago and sell it at $3.80 in New York simultaneously. Arbitrage is what keeps the prices in world markets related to each other.

arbitrageur
One who makes arbitrage transactions for his own account.

art
In general, art as an investment is worth less than art as art. You can lose your shirt buying painters who go out of style, unless you can wait a hundred years until they come back into style. Such things as furniture and gems should not be

relied on for their emergency purchasing power, because in any emergency there may be precious little market for rarities and art works.

ask, ask price, asking price
The price at which an owner is willing to sell.

asset
Something owned by whoever claims the asset. It may not be owned "outright"; there may be debts to be paid off by the owner or claims against it. Assets are listed on the lefthand side of the books of account.

averages
There are about a million business firms in this country. About 100,000 of them have publicly held stocks that can be bought and sold. Most of these actively traded stocks are listed on various stock exchanges or are traded "over the counter." There is no "stock market as a whole," because some prices go up and some go down at the same time. But there are attempts to measure the general drift of things, and these attempts all rest on the assumption that if you measure a few "representative" stocks, your results will say something about the "market as a whole." The oldest and most famous "index" is the Dow Jones Industrial Average (DJIA), which takes an arithmetical average of the prices of thirty stocks—big, old, blue chips (which makes the DJIA far more descriptive of what the blue chips are doing than of what the "market as a whole" is doing). The Federal Reserve Board bases its bond average on Moody's and its stock average on Standard & Poor's. Each stock exchange publishes an index of its own stocks. Several financial publications construct and publish their own indices. Sometimes one major index will go up while another one is going down (this happens, and not rarely, with the DJIA and the Standard & Poor indices). The readings of stock market

averages can be useful in a broad, blunt, approximate way. Don't rely on them for great accuracy, however; and don't trust people who speak in terms of trivial changes (2 percent, 3 percent) in the stock averages. The averages can't be accurate within such close tolerances.

B

backwardation
See **commodities.**

balance of payments
The net of all payments made by American entities and
received by them in dealings with foreign entities. If we
export (sell) more than we import (buy), we have a "trade
surplus." But that can be offset by investment flows,
government payments, and other flows. No country can run
a deficit in its international payments forever. The U.S. has
been running deficits for about twenty years. This is the
root of the "world monetary problem" you read about in
the papers.

balance sheet
The balance sheet is a financial report that shows the
condition of a company at a certain moment in time. The
most common balance-sheet date is the end of the year.
The balance sheet is divided into two main parts: 1) a listing
of all the things the company has "to the good," such as
cash in the bank, inventory for sale, machinery, office
equipment, buildings, payments due from customers; and 2)
a listing of all the things the company "has to make good
on," such as payrolls due, taxes payable, long-term debt
that must be paid back, unpaid bills from suppliers. If the
company has more assets ("to the good") than debts the
difference is called "net worth," and that's what
the stockholders "own," free and clear. If the company has
more debts than assets, it's broke and in deep trouble.

When you're considering investing in a company, study its balance sheet long and hard. Look for a company with plenty of cash—enough to pay off its current debts (those falling due in the next year). Look for total current assets of two or three times total current debts. Look for lots of stockholder equity and a small portion of long-term debt (less than 25 percent of the total capitalization. Look for "inventory" and "work in progress" that aren't out of proportion with total yearly sales volume (which you'll find on the income statement). Keep your eye on the cash. It's one of the few things in accounting that can be measured with absolute accuracy. See also **book value**.

bank

A bank is a sort of scavenging machine. It collects small scraps of cash and consolidates them into a mass of "capital" that can be used for investment. Here's how it works. Suppose you have an income of $1,000 a month, received in equal payments of $250 a week. Suppose you pay your bills once a month, and they add up to $1,000 a month. You're holding your own. Suppose you accumulate your funds by depositing your paychecks in your checking account at the bank. Your *average* bank balance will be $500, day after day. If the bank has a thousand customers, its *average* deposits will be $500,000. The law permits it to assume that this whole sum is *not* going to be drawn out at once; so the bank is allowed to loan out about six times this amount, or $3,000,000. If it earns 15 percent on that amount of loan, the bank earns $450,000 a year. And that's why a relatively small bank can afford to perform all those nice "free" checking services for you. Unless you have definite near-term plans for your cash balances, put them to work in the investment market and start enjoying some of that investment income yourself. Next time you go into your bank, ask one of the officers to show you a recent balance sheet. Add up all the debts the bank owes—

including the **demand deposits** (the balances of the checking accounts "owned" by people like you and me, plus local businesses). Then look at the **cash** on hand, and you'll see that the bank has kept a reserve of only about 16 percent of total deposits. (Actual figures, February 1975: for all commercial banks, about 13,000 of them, cash assets were $105 billion, and total deposits were $709 billion.) The bank is technically busted; it doesn't have enough cash to pay off its depositors. Ask your banker what would happen if everyone wanted cash at the same time. He'll smile. Ask him again. He'll say, "That would never happen." Remind him of 1933 and the runs on the banks. "We have Federal Deposit Insurance now," he'll say with a smug smile. Ask him whether the total cash in the FDIC equals the total unprotected deposits of the banking system. (The coverage is about 5 percent.) He'll suddenly discover an important client he has to talk to, and you're out on your ear. The condition of the banking system is a scandal, a well-kept secret, and a time bomb clicking away in the vaults of the national economy. For this reason, prudent investment managers always like to see their clients holding at least enough cash to see them through about three months of ordinary living expenses if the banks are closed down again.

bankruptcy
You're bankrupt when you can't raise the cash to pay your lawful debts. Laws permit you to declare bankruptcy and seek the protection of legal processes that administer your assets and ration them to your creditors. Corporations can do the same. And the largest corporations are not exempt from bankruptcy.

bear

A bear is someone who thinks the price of a stock, or the stock averages, will go down. He's right, about half the time. Prices are always bouncing up and down in freely negotiated markets, reflecting the arrival of new buyers, new sellers, new products, new problems. There are profits to be made "on the down side." If a bear owns stock, he'll sell it, hoping to buy it back later at a lower price, when the prospects are less "bearish."

He can even live dangerously, if he's a real bear, and sell stock he doesn't yet own. He'll have to borrow the stock in order to deliver what he's "sold," and then hope to buy the stock at a lower price in order to replace the borrowed stock. That will complete the deal.

Bad news is said to be "bearish." A declining market is said to be "a bear market." In financial statuary the bear is always represented as a grizzly—mean and bloody—never a polar, brown, or teddy. And yet we should be fond of him, for he tries to make stock prices as low as possible for us when we want to buy. Doesn't he?

bearer securities

These are securities, usually **bonds,** that are payable to the physical possessor; the owner is not named or registered on any books. A piece of paper money is a bearer security.

bid; bid price

The price at which a buyer is willing to buy. "Bid" and "ask" are the "two sides" of a going market.

Big Board

Shoptalk name for the New York Stock Exchange.

bill rate

The interest rate, figured on an annual basis, for Treasury bills. These "T-bills" are issued at a discount and are redeemed in ninety days at par. The difference between the issue price and the redemption (face value) price is paid as interest. No coupon. The T-bill rate is the most descriptive element of the money-market rate for short-term instruments.

blue chips

In poker or roulette these are the highest-priced chips, thought to be used only by the wealthy, beyond the reach of your penny-ante man. In the stock market, blue chips are companies with proven durability, that have weathered several decades of wars and recessions with strong cash reserves and prospects for continued growth, in keeping with the growth of the national economy. American Telephone & Telegraph paid the same dividend for thirty or forty years, right through the 1930s and the Great Depression. A hundred years from now, General Motors will probably still be building about half the automobiles built in this country. Exxon (formerly Standard Oil of New Jersey— "Esso") will always be a huge factor in the energy business. Eastman Kodak will be in the photographic business forever. Chase Manhattan Bank will keep its share of the banking business for the next hundred years, give or take a percentage point. These are the companies that go up and down with the national economy to some extent, but are large and strong enough to offset some of the worst effects of economic cycles.

However, these companies are so big that they have long since passed the peak period of youthful exuberant growth. They will continue to grow with the economy, the population, and the nominal or unreal "growth" that appears in their financial statements when dollar figures are boosted across the board as a result of monetary inflation. Investors who concentrate in these stocks must be content with investment results that are scarcely better than the long-term growth of the economy in "real" terms. They must be indifferent to the possibility of faster growth in newer and smaller companies, and indifferent to the opportunity for profit in anticipating economic cycles or major economic events such as the devaluation of the currency. And so you find these stocks piled up in huge holdings in pension funds, bank trust departments, insurance companies, foundations, college endowments, mutual funds. You do not find them in the hands of young men and women trying to build their capital quickly. Spectacular profits can be made, on rare occasions, even in the biggest companies; I once bought Exxon for 38 and sold it a couple of years later for 90. But it was more than ten years before I saw another good buying opportunity in that stock! The average portfolio, seeking cash income and long-term gain, should not be too heavy in blue chips. Ten or 15 percent ought to be enough.

board of directors

The people of a company are organizationally divided into three main groups: 1) employees, performing work assigned to them by officers; 2) officers, with broad freedom to design and administer programs whose success or failure may mean promotion or disgrace; 3) directors, who establish general guidelines for the corporation as a whole. The Board of Directors will meet every few months to discuss such questions as raising new funds for expansion, responding to major legal challenges, approving plans to acquire or merge with other companies, voting on whether to distribute additional cash to stockholders as a dividend or to retain it for future use in the business.

A good board will have three kinds of directors: 1) persons with strong experience in the company itself; 2) persons successful in other lines of business whose general experience can be useful to the company in its major decisions; 3) representatives of large holdings of the company's stock. Some companies have nothing but the first type of directors; this is a "company," or "inside" board. A board with too many of the second type is a "figurehead" board, loaded with fancy names, but perhaps a bit short on practical knowledge of the day-to-day work of the company. A company whose officers and directors own most of the stock is "closely held." When you're looking at a company as a possible investment, study the names of the directors. If they're all obscure, or if they're all rather low-placed employees of the firm (assistant treasurer, corporate secretary, director of marketing), you may suspect it's a "captive" board, ready to rubber-stamp any half-baked or fraudulent scheme the officers want to impose. Look for a board that has "outside" members of integrity and judgment, "inside" members whose long-term interests are tightly tied to the long-term interests of the company, and a few representatives of major financial investments in the company. As a general rule, avoid close-held companies, where the interests of the outside stockholders are quite naturally placed in a secondary position. There are exceptions. When a close-held company prepares to "go public" (increase the proportion of its stock held by outsiders), it will do a number of things that make the stock look more attractive, and the price of the stock will rise in the market. Situations like that, if you can find them soon enough in the story, are worth their weight in gold.

bonds

A bond is a legally enforceable claim. To be enforceable, the claim must be defined; so the bond usually carries a promise to repay the loan in certain installments and at certain times, to pay interest at a certain rate on the loan outstanding, and to pledge certain assets or certain income flows as security for the interest payments and/or the loan.

Note that the bondholder (who has loaned cash to the company and who receives the enforceable claim in return) has a very limited interest in the situation. Pay him that fixed amount of interest on time, pay him that fixed amount of repayment of loan on time, and he's happy. His position is radically different from that of the stockholder, who has no fixed claim at all but owns everything that isn't used to repay the debts of the company, and who enjoys all the risks of bankruptcy as well as the rewards of future growth, higher profits, raising dividends, and capital gains on the market price of the stock. The stockholder may hope that the long-term growth of the company will offset some of the damage done by inflation. The bondholder seldom has any protection at all. He gets back a fixed number of dollars, whether those dollars are worth anything or not.

convertible

A convertible bond is a bond that offers the bondholder something other than a fixed number of dollars: the option to purchase a certain number of shares of stock in the same company that issued the bond. The convertible bond will pay interest, of course, and will provide for repayment of the loan; the conversion feature is something extra, usually tossed in to sweeten the deal and make it more saleable to the investing public. Obviously, if the underlying stock is attractive for possible long-term gain, the conversion feature of the bond has some market value in itself, because the option to purchase is exercisable at a stated price. Say the bond (for each $1,000 of face amount) offers the right to purchase twenty shares at $50 a share. If the stock goes to $60 a share, the conversion privilege is worth $200 right there. The bond, then, offers a degree of protection against inflation, but *only* if the underlying stock is genuinely attractive for that same purpose. Convertible bonds are most useful when you use them for high current cash income; the conversion privilege is an additional element that offers you at least some degree of escape from the worst dangers of the bondholder. Caution: do not buy a convertible bond issued by a company whose stock is not attractive in itself.

corporate

A corporate bond is a bond issued by a corporation rather than by a governmental agency, a school district, a criminal on bail, a country club, and so on.

coupon

The amount of interest payable on the bond at a given date, based on the face amount of the bond and expressed in terms of an annual percentage rate. A $1,000 bond carrying a 5 percent coupon is a promise to pay 5 percent of $1,000 in interest per year to the holder of the bond. Everyday conversation: "What's the coupon?" "Five percent."

deep discount

Bonds are usually issued at a price somewhere near par. After that, they are traded in the open market. If the price of the bond falls far below par, the bond is said to sell at a discount. If the discount is more than 30 or 40 percent of par, you'd call it a deep discount. Deep discounts occur when a low-coupon bond issued years ago (to yield, say, 2 percent) is still trading in a market where the general run of interest rates is much higher (say, 10 percent). Deep discounts also can occur when people suspect that a company is going broke.

discount

The difference between par and a lower price.

"E" Series

"E" bonds and similar issues of the federal government have been great disasters for the patriots who bought them. The bonds carried no coupon but were redeemable at successively higher prices year by year. The rise in redemption price expressed an interest rate of 3 percent. The entire bundle of interest accruals was taxable income in the year of redemption. Most people who bought "E" bonds and held them to maturity through a great inflation lost about 30 percent of their original purchasing power.

government (federal)

Government bonds are "good" in that the government will pay them off. But they are "bad" in that the government has the monopoly on creating new money. Historically the government has paid off the old bonds with money that is worth far less than the money it borrowed when it issued the bonds in the first place. This maneuver spares the government the trouble of raising its funds through taxes. The so-called "painless route" of paying off debts with deteriorating currency is always more attractive to the government. But the route is *not* painless. The pain has simply been removed from a visible and measurable place (the income tax return) and transferred to the invisible and immeasurable domains of general price levels, declining purchasing power, and inadequate pension provisions. As a general rule, do not buy government bonds.

government agency

The federal government has been concealing its total debt in recent years by creating more and more agencies with "independent" borrowing power. The Federal National Mortgage Association, the Home Loan Bank, the Federal Land Bank and many other agencies are active borrowers in the money markets. These bonds trade "as if" they were fully backed by the federal government, but they may not be. Avoid them.

index-linked

As inflation progresses, more and more bonds may be defined in terms of some index that measures the buying power of the currency. These indexed bonds are only as good as the issuer's ability to keep pace with inflation. An indexed bond issued by a company that can't raise its prices to match its rising costs is a guaranteed disaster. Some years ago Israel issued bonds linked to the market price of a bag of cement. A more traditional standard would be a bond linked to the market price of gold, or simply a bond promising to pay a certain number of ounces of gold.

market

The bond market is as diffuse as the stock market. Some corporate bonds are listed and traded on the major exchanges such as the New York Stock Exchange and the American Stock Exchange. By far the greatest number of bonds are traded in the over-the-counter market. Government bonds are traded over the counter by a handful of bond houses, financial firms that specialize in maintaining huge inventories of government bonds. Some bonds have an active market. Others may be very difficult to buy or sell. Avoid bonds that don't have an active market.

maturity

"Maturity" is the date on which the borrower promises to fulfill his promise to pay back the original sum (the **principal**) of the loan. A twenty-year bond will have a maturity date that is twenty years later than the issue date.

municipal

Any bond issued by a governmental unit that is not connected with the federal government is called a municipal bond. General obligations of the states; school bonds; sewer bonds; turnpike bonds; hospital bonds; city bonds; county bonds; industrial development bonds—are all municipals. Their most important common feature is that they are exempt from federal income tax. In many cases they are not exempt from other taxes, such as state and city taxes, and they do not, as a rule, have active markets. You can be whipsawed on the difference between bid and ask. For the average investor, the entire field of municipals can be ignored.

par

The par value of a bond is the face amount, the amount due at maturity, the amount originally loaned to the issuer of the bond.

quotes

Bonds are priced, traded, and quoted in terms of percentages of par. A bond with a face amount of $5,000 is quoted at, say, 90. That means you'd pay 90 percent of par for it, or $4,500 (plus commission). The quotes are no better than the market. If the market is inactive, a quote may be far from meaningful. If you have to trade in inactive markets, use **limit orders.** Otherwise you might get a quote of 90, order your broker to buy at the market, and discover to your horror that your order was exercised at 106. It happens. I have seen it. I have not forgotten it.

ratio

The bond ratio in an investment portfolio is the ratio of the market value of bonds to the total market value of the portfolio (bonds, stock, cash, other). The bond ratio (or debt ratio) of a corporation is a balance-sheet ratio of the total bonded debt to the total capitalization (debt plus stockholders' equity). These days, the bond ratio in a personal investment portfolio should be held to the absolute minimum. It is often preferable to liquidate assets rather than to try to live off a fixed income, if the remaining assets are invested in inflation-beating securities. In a corporate balance sheet the bond ratio can vary safely between 60 or 70 percent for a utility and zero for a conservatively capitalized cyclical company.

redemption

Redemption is the issuer's act of paying off the loan. It can occur at the issuer's option or at the bondholder's option, before maturity, in some issues. If you find a particularly attractive bond, make sure the issuer doesn't have the right to redeem it from under you before it runs its full course to maturity!

revenue

A revenue bond is one whose interest payments are due *only* if the current income is high enough to permit payments to be made. Turnpike bonds are typical examples. Some people who thought the revenues of the New Jersey Turnpike were as fixed as the North Star got a surprise when the Arabs quadrupled the price of crude oil. A bond— even an official Turnpike Authority bond backed by the toll booths of the highways—is no better than the underlying economic reality. Don't take anything for granted!

tax-exempt
See **bond: municipal** above.

yield
Yield is the ratio between cash income from an investment
and the capital value of the investment. If you figure the
capital value as your total original cost, then your yield is
yield on cost. If you figure your capital value as the current
market price, then you're computing *current yield.* If you
bought the bond at a discount, and if you figure the
appreciation between the cost price and the ultimate
redemption price as an additional element of income, then
you're talking about *yield to maturity.* But the yield to
maturity is not cash yield, not all of it. Don't buy a bond
simply because the yield is terribly high. It is usually high
because people have doubts about the issuer's ability to stay
in business. The highest yield a bond ever reaches is on the
last interest payment before the company goes broke. Then
the bond falls to zero. Investigate carefully any bond that is
selling at a yield too far above the average.

book value
See **balance sheet.** The book value is also called stockholders' equity. On a typical corporate balance sheet you
would add up all the assets, subtract all the debts, and have
the book value as the remainder. Divide the book value by
the number of shares of stock issued and outstanding, and
you have the book value per share. Because the valuation of
assets may overlook large amounts of current market values,
the book value may often be greatly understated. Because
other assets, such as invisible "goodwill" paid for in
acquiring another company, are hardly of great market
value, you can find cases where the book value is greatly
*over*stated. Book value, therefore, is a tricky and inaccurate
measurement of the worth of a common stock. But if you

develop the ability to adjust the reported book values so that you can compute a company's "real" book value, and if you find the common stock selling at 40 or 50 percent less than the reasonable, hard, common-sense book value, then go ahead and buy the stock. You are probably right.

There is one case where book values are accurate. When the company's assets are almost all tied up in actively quoted and traded securities—as with an investment company, the market value of its portfolio is the total asset of the company, down to the penny. In this case, don't be astonished to find the company's stock selling at a 20 percent discount from the real, visible, accurately computed book value per share. The reason for this is that the investment company may have bought its stocks many years ago, they may have risen greatly in price, and as much as 25 or 30 percent of the market price may be payable in taxes if the company should sell those stocks. So there is an invisible claim against the real and visible market values. Hence the standard discount on the shares of investment companies.

bottoming out
The price drops until it won't drop any further. If it holds at that level through hell and high water and shows signs of trying to start a climb, you can say the price is bottoming out. You can say it—but is it true?

broker
The broker is the man who arranges the details between buyer and seller. A brokerage house makes its money by arranging transactions between buyers and sellers. If you want to buy stock, your broker will find a seller, get an idea of the selling price, make the transaction, handle the delivery of the merchandise, guarantee the genuineness of the goods, provide safekeeping services, send you a statement giving the details of the transaction, and so on. For

this service he charges a fee based on the amount of money involved, the number of shares, and the price per share. I have never understood why the fee schedule had to be so complicated, and I believe that things will be simpler now that brokers are beginning to "negotiate" their fees on a more individualized basis. As a rule of thumb, you can figure the broker's fee, or **commission,** will be about 5 percent on deals involving $1,000 or less, and 1 percent on deals involving $10,000 or more. But if the commission will be an important part of your calculations, be sure to inquire beforehand. (For example, if you buy at 20 hoping to sell at a profit because you *know* the stock will go to 22, don't buy that ticket to Europe until you've figured out whether commissions and other expenses have eaten up the entire gross profit!) There are several hundred brokerage houses and several thousand brokers working in them. When in doubt, ask.

how to pick a broker

The first rule in business is to deal with people who are personally known to you. If you've never dealt with a broker but know one who has been a member of your church or club for ten years, go to him. If you don't know a broker but have a friend who has had satisfactory service from his broker for ten years, go to him. If you don't know anyone who knows a reliable broker, go to the biggest firm in the business: Merrill, Lynch, Pierce, Fenner, and Smith. Call them at their office in the nearest town (they have offices in hundreds of cities) and ask them to set up an account for you. They'll do the rest. But remember: you *must* establish, right off, that you don't want them calling you up with recommendations. Get your advice from someone who doesn't have a vested interest in making trades for the sake of trades.

statements

Each month the brokerage house will send you computerized statements summarizing the transactions made, the securities bought and sold, the cash in and out, and the position (or **balance sheet**) as of the end of the monthly accounting period. You should save these statements, for they constitute a complete record for tax purposes. It will take a little while to learn how to read them, for the computers speak a combination of algebra and Esperanto; but your broker will translate for you until you get the hang of it. Keep your eye on the cash; if that adds up, all else probably will.

bubble

A bubble is a sudden surge of speculation that drives prices to ridiculous heights, from which they fall like hailstones when the bubble bursts. History is rich in bubbles—the South Sea Bubble, the Tulip Craze, the Mississippi Bubble.

There are four sure signs of a bubble, and if you find them all associated with the same event, watch out: 1) rapidly rising prices; 2) widespread interest in the event, with numbers of "investors" who have seldom invested before; 3) general belief that profits will be automatic, universal, infinite, and perpetual; 4) absence of any firm foundation such as a going business, a tangible asset, or measurable prospects underneath the wave of speculation. Of those four factors, the only one that is easily observed by the average investor is, of course, the first one: rising prices. A good general rule, then, is this: don't buy a stock that has recently undergone a tremendous rise in price. I once became interested in a stock that was selling at 14. It looked good, but I noticed that it had run up from 11 in the last few weeks. On investigating, I found that several brokerage houses had been recommending it to their clients at once. I waited. The bubble was small, transient, and relatively harmless. After a few months I bought as much stock as I wanted at prices between 11 and 12. It is at 15 as I write this, and it's solid as a rock.

bucket shop
A low-quality brokerage house. In the old days, it was characteristic for a gang of brokers to get themselves through the day by periodically sending out for a bucket of beer. Don't deal with brokers who drink beer from buckets.

bull
The mortal enemy of the **bear.** A bull thinks prices are going up. He buys now, lest he "miss the ride." He'll "bull" his stocks. He believes only the "bullish" news, and dreams of a "bull market." Since prices go up about as frequently as they go down, the bull has a 50–50 chance of being right. If he enjoys longevity along with exuberance, he may even prosper, because there are some factors that actually work in the direction of long-term bullishness. The natural inventiveness of mankind tends to increase our economic productivity. An increase in productivity amongst a population that is expanding provides the foundation for long-term real economic growth. To that we may add nominal growth in the form of larger and larger numbers describing the same events, as the buying power of the currency declines. There is an institutional bias in the financial business that favors rising prices, simply because brokerage houses find it easier to recommend purchases than sales. In financial statuary the bull is always a black menacing Angus, never a docile Holstein. He paws the ground, horned and horny; his tail whips the air. India has her sacred cows. In the land of the Great Society and other futuristic marvels, we are bemused by the bull.

bullion
Any metal in mass, especially gold and silver, as distinct from coins. See also **gold: bullion** and **silver: bullion.**

bullion coins
Gold and silver coins of no particular rarity, whose trading price is based mainly on the market value of their bullion content. See also **gold: coins** and **silver: coins.**

C

call
The right to buy at a fixed price during a specified period. If a stock is at 70, you might pay $100 for the right to buy the stock at 75 any time in the next three months. That "call" might be worth $500 if the stock moves to 80. The stock moves up 14 percent, while your call moves up 400 percent. Also if you own the stock, you can *sell* a call on it, enhancing your cash flow from the investment. Only about one-tenth of all such calls are ever exercised.

callable bond
A bond that is not guaranteed to run to maturity, where the issuer has the right to "call" the bond, paying a stated price. In the early years, the call price usually involved a slight premium over face value. When you buy a long-term bond for the purpose of putting the money to work, make sure it's not callable.

canned food
See **retreat**. As a "retreat" item, canned food is of course the coming thing. I think all such programs of withdrawing to the forest primeval are long on fantasy and short on common sense.

capital
Capital is whatever you can use to produce income. A carpenter's hammer is part of his capital. The capital of a retail store is invested mainly in its inventory of goods. All capital is created by savings from the current income flow.

It is created by the fact that the owner of the savings has decided to delay, perhaps permanently, spending them on consumer goods. If your savings account at the bank is a permanent factor in your financial situation, then your account balance is your capital, and the interest earned on it is your income. When the general price level is holding steady year after year, the number of dollars in your capital will hold steady if your capital is constant. This seems simple. But when inflation is causing a general rise in prices, the buying power of the dollar keeps going down and down, and it's no longer good enough simply to count the dollars and see if they're holding steady. Millions of Americans are learning that they can no longer make financial plans based on the assumption that the dollar is a reliable and constant measure of real wealth. Without knowing it, millions of other Americans are spending their capital, and gradually impoverishing themselves, because they fail to measure the decline in the purchasing power of the money, and they spend **income** that should actually be saved and added to the capital invested. A simple example: when the money is losing 5 percent of its buying power each year (which is another way of saying the general level of prices is rising by 5 percent a year), a lender will want to get at least 5 percent interest in order to break even. If, in normal times, the usual rate of interest is 3 percent, then the lender will want to charge an interest of 8 percent on his capital. But if he takes the full 8 percent and spends it on his own consumer satisfactions, he's losing ground. He should take that 5 percent and reinvest it. You should too.

There are occasions when you should spend part of your capital: on a wedding, on a child's education, on a major fund appeal from your church, on your final illness. This is also called "invading" your capital. Capital is also called **principal.**

Remember three things: 1) all capital comes ultimately from current savings; 2) savings become capital when the saver decides to treat them as capital; 3) preserving the dollar-amount of your capital won't cut the mustard in times of rapid rises in the general price level.

gain

Capital gain is the same as capital appreciation. See **appreciation.**

market

The capital market, or financial market, is the sum total of everyone who is actively engaged in finding, using, supplying, or creating capital for investment purposes. Capital in this market lives a full life from cradle to grave. It is born in savings institutions where current incomes are carefully accumulated into large sums that find their way into the market for mortgages and government bonds. We see it in adult life as mature capital investments (the stocks of thriving corporations) are bought and sold in millions of daily transfers that don't represent the creation of fresh capital but only changes of ownership. It dies as companies go out of business, cities go broke, bondholders find their investments worth nothing (as has happened in more than six thousand cities in this country over the last two centuries), and inflation subtly undermines the real wealth represented by bonds and savings accounts.

surplus

In accounting, the stockholders' equity in a corporation is the sum of two things: 1) the actual dollar amount of cash paid by the original investors when the stock was originally issued; and 2) the accumulated profits retained in the business. Item number one is divided into two parts: 1) the dollar amount of par value of the shares, usually decided upon by lawyers because each state has different taxes on different par values of newly issued stock; and 2) the excess over par value of the actual selling price of the shares when the original investors subscribe to them. This last item is the capital surplus. It is an accounting and legal term. All you need to know is that the par value plus the capital surplus equals the total cash paid in by the investors who financed the company's stock in the first place.

car

Rent a car or own it? Since the capital market is always working toward coordination of interest rates, the expense of rental will always be pretty close to the income you could earn in the capital market, if you invested in a venture with similar risks. So as a general rule, it's fielder's choice. The deciding factor must be your estimate of what you can earn on your own capital. If you can earn more on your capital than the auto-rental company will charge you for the loan of its capital in the form of a car, then you're ahead of the game to borrow the car and invest the capital in something else. If you do rent a car, you can take advantage of a nice little point: most people don't mind driving a small, cheap, unimpressive car as long as they can say they're just "renting it temporarily." So while you're "thinking of buying a Buick," you can always rent a Pinto— and save a real piece of cash without losing status in the community. See also **home,** where complete financial comparisons are presented.

cash

Cash is money that is immediately spendable. The individual citizen thinks of cash as the money in his pocket. The corporation thinks of cash as its balances in bank accounts, and when you see cash among the assets on a company's balance sheet, that's the common meaning of the word. Everyone, whether individual or corporation, generally tries to keep his cash balances as low as possible in order to liberate as much capital as possible for useful investment (it is the rule that cash earns no interest). Rickenbacker's First

Rule of Financial Analysis proclaims: Keep your eye on the cash. Behind all the complexities and confusions of legal contracts and financial reports, you will always find the bedrock foundation in terms of cash—who pays whom, how much, when, for what, with what strings attached, and from what bank.

equivalent

A cash equivalent isn't as immediately spendable as coin, paper money, or a checking account. With these assets, you can make payments without intermediate steps, but cash equivalent might require you to wait up to a week. A savings account that guarantees withdrawals on short notice would be a cash equivalent. A Treasury bill that trades actively would be a cash equivalent, as would **certificates of deposit** with near-term maturities, **commercial paper** with active markets, and other such instruments.

Corporations try to keep as much cash as possible in cash equivalents, earning some interest income. In analyzing a corporation, it may be useful to find out how much cash is really cash. The Treasurer's job includes keeping the cash at work. International Business Machines runs cash balances of about $4 billion. If the Treasurer can manage to add $500 million to the amount held in cash equivalents at 5 percent a year, his decision will produce an additional income of $25 million for the corporation that year. You can see how a competent Treasurer will earn his pay! It is not well known that most corporations are slow to pay their regular bills. It takes about sixty days for an invoice to a major corporation to get paid. Twenty years ago the lag was a month. Suppose your bills are $1 billion a month and you manage to "stretch" your payables to an average of two months. You have "freed up" exactly $1 billion for investment in cash equivalents. But that is corporate finance. For the average citizen the savings accounts and time deposits are the most available cash equivalents.

flow

In corporate finance "cash flow" is the total cash receipts in a given period, minus total cash expenditures. It differs from net profit because it includes certain "charges" that are accounted for even though they do not represent current expenditures of cash. **Depreciation** is the most common example. If your capital equipment is good for ten years and then must be replaced, you are wise to "allow" for this as a charge against profits by "writing off" about one-tenth of the cost of the capital equipment each year (in practice the formula is terribly complicated). Roughly, cash flow is retained profits plus depreciation charges. It's an important figure because it tells you how much cash is available for meeting interest-payment obligations, retiring the debt, paying preferred dividends, meeting rental obligations, and so on. Airlines have extremely high cash flows in relation to their profits. Service industries, with relatively small amounts of capital equipment, have cash flows that are about the same as their retained profits.

reserves

Every citizen, whether investor or not, should have some cash reserves. These should be as small as possible, but large enough to meet the routine obligations of life plus the emergency demands of "the rainy day." We all maintain a certain small amount of pocket currency, probably about enough to take care of one week's out-of-pocket expenses. The checking account should be kept only high enough to avoid bank service charges and penalty charges (but do study the calculations in **checking account** below). The savings account should be used for storing up larger amounts of money for infrequent expenses such as vacations, large purchases, and down payments.

"Emergency reserves" should be held in various forms and should be enough to pay the bills for two or three months (just in case the banking system should shut down again in this country as it did a few decades ago). The various forms of emergency reserves should be 1) folding money, 2) circulated silver dollars, and 3) twenty-dollar gold pieces. The folding money will gradually lose buying power as the inflation continues, but the silver dollars and the gold coins will gradually (perhaps, on occasion, rapidly) gain in market price as the inflation continues, and the gains may go a great way toward offsetting the loss on the paper currency. Why hold any paper currency at all? Because you'll have to have something to live on while you're trying to maneuver through the chaos and find a decent market for your silver and gold coins. How likely is it that we'll go through another phase of bank closings? I'd say the chance is slight in the next few years, but real enough to make me think a reserve of three months' expenses is not too much.

Beyond these reserves, the average investor should also maintain a "buying reserve" in his portfolio. This varies from time to time, sometimes going as high as 30 percent of market value, sometimes as low as 5 percent. But I like to see at least *some* buying power in an account at all times, simply because it permits the investor to take advantage of opportunities that may appear on the investment horizon without warning. This store of buying power can be thought of as "idling capital," capital that is not doing work, but is nevertheless useful because it is holding itself available. Its engine is idling, ready for immediate service when wanted. And it's performing a real service by keeping itself ready to perform quickly. Amazingly few people understand this idea.

cats and dogs

Low-priced stocks of inferior breeding. Small companies, no earnings, unknown management, questionable outlook, no sponsorship. Avoid 'em like the plague.

certificate (stock)

The stock certificate is the piece of paper that testifies that you are the owner of so many shares in such-and-such corporation. It's printed on heavy paper, issued by a transfer agent, signed by a couple of officers, and more often than not has a bosomy woman seated on a globe or a large grapefruit holding a sceptre, facing a stiff breeze, and smiling confidently. I once knew a lady who, because blue was her favorite color, bought nothing but stocks from companies who printed their certificates in that color. She did very well indeed with her investments. If you hold stock certificates rather than owning shares in street name, get a safe deposit box and put the certificates there. You can replace a lost certificate if need be, but the administrative labor of doing so is fearsome.

certificate of deposit (CD)

The CD is a security issued by a bank stating that it has borrowed money from you and will pay it back with interest at a certain time. CDs pay high interest but come in units of $100,000 or so.

charge account

Try to do as much of your business as possible with charge accounts. Gas stations, drug stores, many food markets, newsstands (if you're a regular), and all sorts of businesses will take you on as a charge-account customer if you're a resident, a regular client, and a reliable personality. The great advantage of opening up charge accounts is that they permit you to pay next month for what you acquire this month. They "free up" one month's expenses and give you that much to put to work as capital. If you can add $1,000 to your investments by doing this, and if you can earn 20 or 30 percent a year on your portfolio, we're talking about a good thing. Be sure, though, that you do pay on time. Many stores will charge you a penalty of about 18 percent a year on late payments. It's not worthwhile to "borrow" at that rate if, at the same time, you're destroying your reputation in the community by getting into the habit of neglecting your bills. Utility companies, however, will often let you go two or three months overdue without charging a penalty. If your phone bill runs into many hundreds of dollars a month, it might be worthwhile to set up a regular routine of paying exactly one month late. But unless the amounts are worthwhile, don't jeopardize your standing.

chart
A map. On Wall Street, commonly misused to mean graph. The graph shows changes in stock prices, with the implication that it has predictive powers, which it doesn't. See also **random walk.**

checking account
Most banks offer two kinds of checking accounts, the special and the regular. You should study your own needs carefully and see whether you can "free up" some capital from this source. Here's an example. The bank charges $0.08 for each check you write, $0.03 for each check you deposit, and $1.50 per month carrying fee. In an average month you deposit fifteen checks, write forty-one checks, and keep an average balance of $1,000 in the account. The bank's charges for that month will be $5.23. However, the bank allows you a credit, against those charges, of $0.30 for each $100 kept in the account for the whole month. You will have to keep $1,743 on deposit for the month in order to "earn" that $5.23. That works out to a yearly rate of interest earned on your capital of only 3.6 percent! You could do far better by maintaining almost no balance in the checking account and investing the $1,700 in a good portfolio with current income and some prospect of long-term gains. Then just pay the bank for the services it

renders. What other business will perform, for a few pennies, speedily and accurately, a transaction that may span the continent? It's a bargain.

children
Each state has different laws, but it's possible in every state to make gifts of securities to children who are not of age by appointing an adult (usually a parent) as guardian or custodian. No legal expenses involved. A brokerage house will set up the account for you. Then your children can get started building their own financial careers. Income earned on their capital is taxable to them, not to you. (If you transfer more than $60,000 to any one child, you may run the risk of paying gift taxes; ask a lawyer about that point.) Remember that the custodian arrangement automatically ceases when the child comes of age. You might not want to set this kind of thing up for children who don't show signs of being able to handle things wisely. But there's nothing that can quite match the feeling children have when they first realize they own a small piece of the productive machinery that keeps this country going. That's when they begin to "put it all together." And if you start them soon enough and the portfolio is managed well, they may be able to finance their own college years, provide capital for their own small businesses, or make a down payment on a house.

Christmas Clubs
Many banks offer a Christmas Club plan that allows you to make regular deposits throughout the year and receive the total balance in the Christmas season for your yearly beneficences and surprises. Trouble is, the greatest gift you're giving is to the bank, which has the use of your money for almost a year—and in too many cases, doesn't pay you anything near the going rate of interest. One common plan provides for your making forty-nine weekly deposits and the bank contributing the fiftieth weekly

deposit itself, which works out to slightly more than 4 percent interest on the average amount "invested." Unless you can do as well as in a regular savings account, forget it. Christmas is for your friends, not for the local banker!

churning

Churning is excessive and harmful trading activity in your portfolio. Unscrupled brokers will try to talk you into buying and selling stocks at such a dizzy pace that the commissions eat you up. If there's a great deal of activity in an account, and the account is not making any money for the investor, you should suspect the broker of willfully churning the account to create commissions for himself. A well-managed long-term account should be quite inactive. Its "turnover"—the ratio of dollar amount of total transactions to dollar amount of average market value—may be about 10 percent. An active and successful speculator may have a turnover of 100 percent a year. A churned account could be anything—500 percent, 600 percent—but the warning symptom is absence of results. The really fine profits from investments are made by buying well and then hanging on for the long pull. Churn not, weep not.

clearing

A "clearing house" matches up all buy and sell orders handled for its members and sends them a check or an invoice for the net amounts due after the arithmetic is settled. Banks, commodity exchanges, and stock exchanges all operate clearing houses, or are members of clearing organizations.

climax

A climax is seen in stock markets when a long bull market ends with a tremendous burst of buying that drives prices into irrational orbits, or when a long bear market ends with a "selling climax" that knocks the stuffing out of almost everything. More easily identified in hindsight. High volume of trading is the warning signal. General rule is to avoid trading when the volume is at unusual levels.

closed-end vs. open-end
See **mutual funds.**

collateral
Stocks and bonds may be used as collateral for loans. You can usually borrow about 60 percent of the market value of listed stocks and more than that on bonds.

commemoratives
The federal government used to issue coins, usually fifty-cent pieces, honoring men and women and occasions of perhaps something less than national importance. These coins have skyrocketed in price, simply because they were not issued in the astronomical quantities of a mint run destined for general circulation. In the last ten years, a different sort of commemorative has come into prominence—the "medallion" issued by privately owned businesses. These artifacts, coins, medals, dinner plates, and so on are made of silver, and are sold on the basis of 1) their bullion content, and 2) their scarcity, for they are "limited editions," supposedly on their way to becoming "collector's items." There are troubles here. The selling price of these objects is usually two or three times the market value of the silver or gold bullion they contain. And there is little evidence that scarcity alone creates rising prices—there must also be demand; the five-leaf clover is exceptionally scarce, and dirt cheap. Such "investments" as a matched set of butter plates honoring Buster Keaton do more honor to Mr. Keaton than to the buyer. These things are not "stores of value" unless you can rely on an active secondary market for them, especially in times of emergency. You'd be better

off buying the stocks of the companies that manufacture these intentionally scarce "collector's items."

commercial paper
Short-term IOUs issued by blue-chip companies. Traded in rather active markets. Interest rates very attractive. Available in rather big chunks only.

commission (broker)
A stock broker will charge a commission when he arranges a purchase or sale for you. In a small transaction, the commission can be as high as 6 percent of the money and less than 1 percent in a larger transaction. A good rule of thumb is to figure that you'll burn up 3 percent of your money in a round trip (purchase and subsequent sale of the same block of stock).

commodities
Raw materials, both natural and industrial, including metals: lead, platinum, silver, gold, and so on; produce: eggs, soybeans, wheat, corn, pork bellies (the raw material of the bacon processor), barley, and hundreds of other products. Businesses that need a steady supply of raw materials seek to assure themselves of future supplies at a predictable price. That demand for a guaranteed future price is satisfied by free-market forces that maintain warehouses, issue warehouse receipts, operate clearing houses to match up sales and purchases of receipts, operate commodity exchanges for trading in contracts for future delivery, and so on. Commodity trading is active, specialized, fascinating, and perilous. I strongly disapprove of it for the average investor, if for no other reason than that the smallest amount you can trade is usually $5,000 or $10,000.

backwardation

Backwardation occurs when the prices for future deliveries are progressively lower than the going market price of the commodity.

contango

The opposite of backwardation, a contango market exists when the future prices of a commodity are progressively higher than the going market price.

contract

A contract, or option, or future, is a binding agreement to deliver a specified quantity of a given commodity, of specified purity, at a specified time, in a specified place. Only a small fraction of the purchasers of commodity futures actually take delivery of the physical commodity itself.

futures

See **commodities: contracts** above.

option

See **commodities: contracts** above.

conglomerates

A conglomerate is a company that's active in a variety of unconnected industries. One large conglomerate is in financial services, consumer products, movies, mining, and manufacturing. Given the difficulties of accounting for even the simplest operations (how much is a factory worth?), what are you to think of a company that lumps dissimilar operations together and comes up with a single number at the bottom of the page: earnings per share? The answer is: Keep a prudent distance. It is not that everyone in conglomerates is a swindler, but it is true that complexity is the hunting ground of the sharpy. Simply because it's so difficult to evaluate the balance sheet and the income statement of a full-fledged conglomerate, the market price of the stock is subject to irrational forces to a far greater degree than the stock of a straightforward operation such as a blue-jeans manufacturer or an air-freight forwarder. Conglomerates, too, usually own interests in subsidiary corporations, and it's often impossible to "keep your eye on the cash" of the subsidiaries; trouble may be building up for years, invisibly. Remember, conglomerates don't spring to life like mosquitoes after rain. They are built to be intentionally complicated. They do not serve your purpose as an investor, because your purpose is to have as clear an idea as you possibly can about what's happening to your money.

constant dollar
Because of inflation, the dollar is *not* constant. It's as if we had a tape measure that was a yard long, thirty years ago, and is now a foot long. If you bought one tape of fabric thirty years ago and one tape now, you would have "two tapes" of fabric now, but would your fabric be six feet long or two feet long? Thirty years ago, a dollar would buy about three times as much physical goods as it does now. If you bought a dollar's worth thirty years ago and a dollar's worth now, you have two dollars' worth now, but would you have twice as much physical goods as you had before the second purchase? Such questions become serious practical problems during a serious inflation, when you're studying the financial records of a company over a long period of years. It is necessary to adjust the reported figures in order to take into consideration the vastly changed meaning of the dollar. The measuring unit must be made standard—same size, same meaning, year after year. The adjusted unit is called the "constant dollar." The problem never existed when the currency was defined as a certain number of ounces of a metal, such as gold. The buying power of gold tends to

remain amazingly constant. Forty years ago a good business suit in New York City cost the same as an ounce of gold. In 1976 it still does. If our money were the "ounce" (or the "pound"), the problem of converting to a constant value would quietly go away.

constant ratio

Formula investment plan that provides for periodic sales and purchases so that the ratio of bonds and stocks (at market value) will not vary too far from the desired ratio. Applying a constant ratio controls the amplitude of fluctuations through a price cycle (the higher the bond ratio, the lower the amplitude), but has no effect at all on portfolio performance from one peak to the next peak. There's a mathematical formula that proves it.

Consumer Price Index

The so-called "cost-of-living" index prepared by the federal government; it purports to describe the experience of an average family, yet everyone seems to think that prices are rising even faster than the CPI. One problem of the CPI is that it ignores the quality of goods and services. If price remains constant but quality declines, we *feel* it as a price rise, but the CPI doesn't report it as such.

contango
See **commodities.**

contrarians

Ancient wisdom says: "Don't fight the tape." Don't try to oppose the combined financial resources of the rest of the world, as reported on the ticker tape. If the entire market is crashing and continues to crash day after day, why should you be the hero who wades in and buys? Well, for every bit of ancient wisdom there's a bit of maverick mania, and the contrarians exist for the purpose of fighting the tape. They say that by the time the news is known by everyone, it's obsolete; therefore mass buying and mass selling are always wrong, and you need only know what the majority is doing to make your fortune by doing the opposite. This is simple-minded. At bottom it's an attempt to escape responsibility for your own decisions. You must ignore your own opinions and wait for the majority to express its, a peculiarly inert and unassertive attitude to adopt in the management of a financial portfolio. Avoid all such systems of mechanical decision-making. Or, better still, study their results; and then avoid them.

convertible securities
Some bonds and preferred stocks carry the right to "convert" into a certain number of common shares (sometimes upon the payment of additional money). This right acquires market value when the "underlying" common stock rises so much in price that it forces the convertible security to rise also. Conversion *parity* is the market value of the convertible instrument divided by the number of shares it can be converted into. Conversion *premium* is the difference between parity and the market price of the stock.

corner
You have a corner on the market, or you have cornered the market, when you have acquired the whole floating supply of a stock or commodity. After that, no matter how high the price is bid, there will be no sales unless you desire to sell. Corners are fun in theory, and they're great targets for the critics of liberty, but in actual practice they're unimportant and short-lived, as well as illegal nowadays. The late elder Gulbenkian once cornered the world market in pepper. He owned or controlled a billion-year supply for his own table. It was obvious that he could not use or enjoy that supply. He would sooner or later be required to sell it in order to do

something more sensible with his funds. In due course he sold, making a slight profit—10 or 15 percent—and that was that. Even the Arabs have learned that a corner is not the same as wealth. They cannot eat oil, or live in it, or wear it. They are required to sell it at a price that meets the competition of other forms of energy and other sources of oil. If the forces of the market are allowed to operate, these problems dry up and blow away surprisingly soon.

corporation
A "person" under the law, a corporation has an eternal life. Its owners are not personally responsible for its acts, but its officers and directors are. Ownership may be acquired or disposed of (through transactions in the stock) without consulting management, whereas the approval of the partners is necessary to enter or withdraw from their partnership. The corporate form of organization permits the accumulation of capital that is at the heart of economic productivity. Ownership is represented by shares of stock.

costs: fixed vs. variable
Fixed costs are the same for any given time period: rent, salaries, interest payments, depreciation. Variable costs are the same for each unit of work accomplished: materials, hourly labor, shipping. In studying a company, bear in mind that the higher the fixed costs, the more speculative the investment. Try to find companies with "collapsible" operations, companies that can draw in their horns when the going gets rough. During the worst of years, these will survive and may even continue to show profits.

cost of credit
See **interest.**

counsel (investment)
See **advice.**

coupon
   See **bond.**

coverage
Fixed obligations, such as interest payments or preferred-stock dividends, are more certain if they're only a small portion of the income flows available for such payments. So the ratio between fixed charges and funds available for them is important in evaluating the quality of the obligations. Coverage is that ratio—the number of times the fixed charges are earned. It can be figured before tax, after tax, or on the basis of cash flow. It should include leasehold obligations when necessary.

credit cards
If you believe in cash on the barrelhead, you'll probably think credit cards are positively immoral. And yet they're scarcely different from money itself; they simply arrange for the means of payment. When you use a credit card, you are issuing a promise to pay. If you issue that promise when you know you have neither the means nor the intention of paying—well, *you're* immoral, not the little plastic card. For the rest of us, credit cards permit us to defer payment for a month or so, and that permits us to liberate another batch of capital from the non-earning cash account and put it to work in an income-producing investment.

creeping inflation
Properly speaking **inflation** is *any* increase in the money supply. There is no definite measurement of creeping inflation. I think that the common understanding is that creeping inflation is an inflation that proceeds at a constant pace slow enough to be safely ignored by the vast majority of the people. We've had almost constant inflation in this country since its discovery by those great inflationists, the

Spaniards. Another definition of creeping inflation might be this: inflation that causes such a rapid rise in the price level that existing contractual relationships are disturbed or disrupted. We have been well beyond the creeping phase since the mid-1960s. Millions of Americans are discovering that a savings account, a bond, an insurance policy, a guaranteed pension, will no longer do the work originally anticipated.

cumulative preferred stock
A preferred stock has first dibs on money available for common dividends. If the money isn't available in one year, and if the dibs are cumulative, then the money remains due and payable, cumulatively, out of future funds available for that purpose. Unpaid cumulative dividends are *arrearages*, and sometimes there are happy hunting grounds amongst preferreds in arrears when corporate reorganizations or resurrections make it likely that the arrearages will be cleaned up. Don't play that game unless you have special knowledge.

Curb
The American Stock Exchange, called so because in olden days business was conducted on the street, with clerks sitting in windows taking reports of the trades by hand signals. Ain't that romantic?

currency
Hand-to-hand money is currency. There is a popular assumption that the currency of the United States is in the banks, and that we can "cash in" our bank accounts for currency at any time. A recent tabulation should open a few eyes:

checking accounts	$ 215 billion
time deposits and savings deposits	429 billion
deposits at non-bank thrift institutions	375 billion
TOTAL DEPOSITS	$1,019 billion
currency and coin held by banks	8 billion

Numbers such as these are what I have in mind when I urge investors to keep a little something stashed away as an emergency reserve. The entire American banking system *could* collapse. It doesn't have enough cash on hand to pay even one cent on the dollar to its depositors. "Keep your eye on the cash!"

current assets
Assets in sufficiently liquid form to be used in payment of current liabilities.

current liabilities
Debts due and payable within twelve months.

current ratio
Current assets divided by current liabilities.

customer's man
See **broker.**

cycles
In nature nothing moves in straight lines. There are ups and downs, the waves rising and crashing as the tide comes in or goes out, but always the waves. In business we see similar patterns. A *complete* cycle would carry you back to your starting point. If the long-term trend is up or down, a cycle

might not make it back to the starting point, but it would be close enough to give you the idea. There are lots of different cycles, and they require different responses from the investor.

civilization

There are theories of the rise and fall of whole civilizations and cultures. These cultural cycles happen so slowly that they need not concern the average investor. If you had been living in Rome in the fifth century when Alaric was at the gates, you could have survived very nicely by switching your investments from vineyards to cargo ships.

company

An individual company may undergo its own cyclical pattern. Every company starts at zero and—if it is to survive—enjoys an initial growth rate that seems astronomical. After ten years or so, the company usually settles down to a growth rate of 10 or 20 percent a year. After another period of ten years or so, it settles down to a rate of 5 or 10 percent a year (in real terms, with nominal growth added on).

Within this general pattern of new companies you can define a couple of cyclical patterns at work. One is the result of management changes. A new cycle will start when a new management team takes over. It may be a good or a bad cycle depending on the ability of the new team. The other factor is innovation. A company may have a new gizmo that works for fifteen years—until the patent runs out, a new super-gizmo is introduced, or the fashions change. Then, unless it can bring out a new widget to follow the gizmo, the cycle is completed and the company is back to the starting line. Some companies, through intense concentration on research and development, manage to maintain a steady ratio of new products in their total sales. One of the great innovators is "3M"—Minnesota

Mining and Manufacturing. Each year this fine company manages to get 20 percent of its business from products it has introduced within the last five years, and it keeps that ratio year after year for decades. When you're looking at a company, try to find one like 3M that will promise to push into the frontier of new products. This will assure you of investments in a strong mixture of products in the early and fast-growing phases of their cycles. If you can't find companies like that at prices you can tolerate, try to find a company with one or two products, or a company itself in the early stages of the cycle. Examples would be office equipment in the 1930s, airlines in the 1940s, air freight in the 1950s, gold shares in the 1960s, and perhaps gold and silver shares again in the 1970s.

country

Nations undergo their own kinds of cycles. For example, you would not want to invest in a country that is slipping into the hands of Communists, while you *would* want to invest in one determined to protect the freedom of the individual and the institution of private property. If you have all your investments in one country, you should occasionally take a long-range view of the situation to make sure you're not riding a dying horse. Even though you may wish to keep your assets concentrated in U.S. corporations, you might look into each company it owns shares in, and see if there's too much capital invested in countries of questionable political outlook.

industry

Industry groups have their own cycles, too. The discovery of petroleum sent the whaling industry into a long decline while setting the stage for long-term growth in the petroleum industry. The television manufacturers were all prospering while the television industry was young. The growth was so rapid that there was plenty of room for everyone. A wise investor would have understood that "the tree does not grow to the sky," and would have sold out and taken his profits before the industry ran into saturated markets, cut-price competition, and changing fashions. The investor should try to keep the bulk of his investments in industries that have long-term prospects. And let me emphasize that long-term aspect. I do not mean something like two years for double-knits or one year for a blockbuster film from RKO, but something with broad and growing appeal to whole populations, a product based on some fundamental aspect or trend of human life such as a growing acceptance of soybean additives in human food, a permanent increase in the use of denims, a long-term and universal trend toward monetary inflation. Find these trends and the industry groups that serve the new needs arising from them. Find good companies that stand to benefit from these new markets. And *voilà!*

national economy

The "business cycle" is measured by statistics based on the national economy as a whole: cycles in unemployment rates, interest rates, corporate profits, average hours in the work week, and so on. Critics of the system of free-market allocation of capital declare that the business cycle is an inherent disease of free markets. However elaborate research in historical statistics discloses that the business cycle is caused by variations in the money supply, which is not in the hands of the free market, but is controlled by governments (in the U.S., by the Federal Reserve Board). This explains why the ups and downs of the business cycle have been more extreme in the years since the creation of the Federal Reserve Board. It also provides an opportunity for you, as an investor, to foresee the ups and downs of the business cycle. If you follow the workings of the Federal Reserve System closely enough, you should be able to spot the times when the "Fed" is going through one of its typically abrupt switches from "easy money" to "tight money," or vice versa. It is these switches that cause the boom-and-bust cycle in the national economy. Look for a sudden and sharp increase in the rate of growth of the money supply. Within six months the stock market will start rising. The pattern is observable as far back as you care to investigate the statistics.

D

day order
An order to buy or sell at a stated price; valid only for the day you give the order to your broker.

debenture bonds
Bonds whose interest is due only if earned, or only from certain specified sources; bonds that are not a *general* obligation of the issuer.

debt
The amount borrowed.

debt ratio
Amount borrowed (and due beyond twelve months) as a percentage of total capital (debt and equity together).

defensive stocks
The defensive investor pays little attention to the possibility of profit. His main worry is to avoid loss. It is normal and intelligent for elderly investors to put a high value on defensive investing, simply because, if they make a mistake in their old age, it is no longer possible for them to recoup their fortunes. In recent decades the typical defensive stocks have been public utilities, large retail chains, and tobacco companies. A couple of generations ago the most defensive stocks were those of the street railway (trolley) companies. Before that it was railroads and still earlier, insurance companies and banks. But one after another these industries have ceased to protect the buying power of the

investor's capital. In times of rapid inflation it is not enough to hold your own in dollar terms. You must make profits—capital gains—in order to break even! Hence the defensive strategy that works in stable times is obsolete when the counting system (the currency unit) has gone out of whack. The most speculative holding, during inflation, is solid cash, the most defensive strategy is maximum long-term gain, and the most difficult objective is to maintain the buying power of current investment income. Elderly investors must still invest defensively, but they must learn that the line of defense has shifted. It is no longer the protection of the starting capital expressed in face-amount dollars. The *buying power* of their capital is what they must defend, because that's what's under attack when the government inflates the money supply, thus undermining the buying power of the currency. A typical defensive strategy would be this: set the minimum cash income requirement; secure this cash income with high-**yield** stocks; put everything else into stocks with the best prospects for long-term growth; and pray, because the historical record shows that there is no easy or automatic solution to the financial problems caused by governmental money mismanagement.

deflation

Any decrease in the money supply. Naturally it causes a drop in the general level of prices. The Federal Reserve, during the 1930s, caused a 30 percent drop in the money supply, with consequences that are usually blamed on "business." There is nothing demonic in deflation, just as there is nothing sacred in inflation. Under conditions of freedom, with all costs (including the cost of wages) flexible and responsive to market trends, a decrease in the money supply leads to immediate and proportionate decreases in prices and wages, and relative positions will be undisturbed (with the exception of fixed-income contracts, which will be favored on the side of those receiving the money that enjoys increased buying power). Deflation and inflation upset the terms of contracts denominated in money units, and upset the conditions of the market when those conditions are made rigid through governmental edict (minimum wage, maximum price, licensing cost, and so on). The principal message for the investor is that deflation leads to lower prices. When you suspect we're in for a deflation (even a temporary or mild one of six months, merely stabilized rather than increasing money supply), you should reduce your holdings in common stocks on the chance of buying back in at significantly lower prices a few months later. During the 1960s and 1970s, this kind of thing has been happening every two or three years. It's worth watching for.

deflator
A statistical device, more accurate than the CPI. Used in correcting dollar figures for the effects of inflation.

demand deposit
A deposit in a bank. You have the right to withdraw, in currency or by bank draft, without advance notice. Few people know that most savings accounts are *not* demand deposits, but that savings banks have the legal right to require advance notice (sometimes ninety days) of the depositor's intent to withdraw funds.

depletion
What happens when you mine a natural deposit of ore, petroleum, gems. It doesn't represent income but a return of original capital. Accounting entries, which are basically estimates of the useful life of the mine, permit charges against income in the form of depletion allowances.

depreciation

Depreciation is what happens when you buy a piece of equipment that will be serviceable in your business for more than one year: its market value drops steadily (depreciates) by about 20 percent in the first year (basically a result of the salesman's commission). It then depreciates slower, until at some future moment it's worth no more than what it might bring from the scrap dealer. Viewed from the standpoint of the machine's entire life, a "cost" has been incurred, a "loss" of the machine's market value, down to the residual or scrap price.

How should you show this loss on your books of account and on your income and expense statements? If you are on the cash basis of accounting—showing only those transactions that take place for cash—then you can't show this loss, because it's not a cash transaction until that final accounting period when you sell the worn-out machine to the junk dealer. Then you would take the entire loss in that one accounting period. Yet there is something that says this isn't a realistic way to express the loss, for it didn't, after all, occur all at once, but little by little over the years. So the accountant strives to spread the loss around, allowing a little of it in each year. Therefore, the "depreciation allowance" of the accountant is a non-cash charge against reported earnings. It is an attempt to express the real events of the period, even when those events took place without any cash changing hands. You will find depreciation stated separately in the income statement. On the balance sheet you will find each depreciable asset of the company stated separately and usually as follows: the original purchase price, minus the "reserve" for accumulated depreciation, giving the "net book value" of the asset.

If a company has held its assets long enough to "write them off" almost entirely down to scrap value, then you have an interesting situation, good or bad, that should be investigated further. It might mean that the company is operating with terribly obsolete equipment and must raise money in the capital markets in order to retool for the next round of technological competition (in the past, this has been the ruinous pattern of the airplane-crazed airlines). Or it might mean that the company has "written off" the assets well ahead of their normal retirement age, the **book value** of the company is grossly understated, and the company is concealing large amounts of market values in its "net" asset valuations on the balance sheet. (This is useful information particularly when the company's assets are marketable in a variety of ways—as, for example, a company with a large library of feature films that could be exhibited in foreign countries, on television, in reruns, and so on.) The tax laws allow a very complicated system of depreciation charges. Many companies take one form of depreciation write-off for tax purposes and a different write-off for purposes of reporting to stockholders. There's nothing indecent or unethical about that; there's no reason why the tax law should be the best guide for describing the economic results of a business operation. But, if you see a tax liability that is totally out of harmony with the published taxable income, be on the lookout for accounting tricks that may be overstating the good news to the stockholders. And if the stock is selling at an extremely high price, exercise extreme caution. It might mean slickers at work. See also **cash flow.**

depression
There's no exact definition of an economic depression. It's a more severe episode than a recession, but the cause is the same in both cases—a drop in the money supply as managed by the government. The results are unemployment, falling profits, business failures, and falling prices—rendered even more painful if there are existing programs or laws that prohibit the economy from responding swiftly and adequately to the new situation. For example, it is widely over-

looked that individuals and businesses routinely respond to rising or falling prices and have done so throughout history, but that the concepts of recession and depression are tied exclusively to economies that use money created by government monopoly. In non-money economies there are no booms or depressions. There is simply full employment and steady operational systems. In money economies (where the money supply is regulated by free-market forces) imbalances in the money supply are corrected by swift and sharp moves (called *panics* or *fevers*). Governmental control of the money supply was introduced in an effort to correct the sudden sharp moves, and has brought about a system of long and agonizing corrections instead. Before the start of the Federal Reserve System, the average correction (after an overissue of currency) took a few weeks. Now it takes several months, and in the 1930s it took years. Indeed, the word "depression" did not come into existence in this meaning until *after* the founding of the Federal Reserve System.

Depressions can be survived. The investor may even make huge profits during a depression, as the late Joseph Kennedy did. All you need do is keep an eye on the money supply and be prepared to sell out before the money starts shrinking. Pay off your debts. Make loans to prime credits. Sell cyclical stocks short. Keep a strong cash reserve ready for buying at the bottom. And when will the bottom arrive? When the money supply has leveled off for three to six months. These rules assume markets that are relatively free to adjust themselves to new conditions. If the government has pickled everything in price freezes and regulations, the conditions of recession may last forever, as they do in socialized economies around the world.

diamonds
Not recommended as investments, diamonds are useful principally because they compress a huge amount of buying power into a small space and permit transportation of capital. But there's a huge loss in transaction costs, danger of misplacement, and difficulty of assay, subdivision, and so on. Good emergency money for escaping across national boundaries. But—whither to flee with the ice?

dilution
A thinning down. When convertible securities are converted into the common stock the number of shares of stock increases, and the earnings are spread over a larger number of shares, reducing the reported earnings per share.

directors
People who are responsible for the overall policy of corporations. They meet every few months, review the general situation, and set broad guidelines for future policy. See also **board of directors** and **corporation.**

discounting
In financial jargon to discount means to strike a price today based on your future estimates. (See **anticipation.**) Stock prices are also said to "discount" good news or bad news; the market is said to "discount" the election. In this sense to "discount" may involve a move upward as well as downward. But in the more normal use of the word, a discount is a reduction in price, as when during a period of rising interest rates, a bond sells below its par value.

The "discounting function," which permits the suppliers and users of capital to determine where the need is greatest, is the great service provided by freely functioning financial markets. In economies where there is no such market, there is no rational way to determine where fresh capital should

be applied in order to respond to the greatest needs of the
population. In a centrally planned economy, a bankrupt
enterprise may have the same credit standing as an
enterprise showing a profit. Misallocation of capital is
inevitable, and the index of productivity will decline.
Hence the need to trade with countries such as the U.S.,
where capital is allocated more efficiently, thanks to the
discounting function of the capital markets.

discretionary account

If you have power to act in your own name, you can sign a
power of attorney that will give someone else the power to
buy and sell stocks and bonds for your account without
getting your specific approval for each recommendation.
Many people make use of these so-called discretionary
accounts. An investor who decides he cannot make useful
decisions will subcontract those decisions by giving discretionary authority to someone else. A man who is too busy to
be bothered, or who travels so much that he can't be sure
he'll be on hand when a decision is needed, will often find it
useful to set up a discretionary account. In practice it is
unwise to give discretionary authority to a broker, because
you create an unavoidable conflict of interest. The broker's
interest is in **churning** your account; your interest is in
buying well and holding long. Independent advisers take
discretionary accounts, and any brokerage house will be
glad to take orders from an adviser who has power to act in
his client's name. The adviser should not charge you
anything extra for managing a discretionary account;
indeed he should charge you more for *not* having discretion,
because then he is obliged to pursue and persuade you
every time he wants to do something for your benefit.

As a broad general rule, discretionary accounts show
better market performance than non-discretionary accounts. If you start using an adviser, you might work with
him for a few months until you have a good idea of his

methods and results. If everything works smoothly, you can eventually give him discretionary power, and then all you do is sit back and watch the results come in. A half-way house is not uncommon: you can give discretionary authority to your adviser, but you can order your broker not to take action on your adviser's orders until a certain number of days have passed. This will give you time to receive a copy of your adviser's order to your broker to veto it if necessary. This system is less cumbersome than it may sound. You can cancel a discretionary power at any time and on a moment's notice. All transactions in a discretionary account must be initiated on the basis of written orders, and brokers are glad to send duplicate notices to clients and advisers. It's a system well worth looking into.

Don't pay more than 1 percent of market value per year for such services. There are sharks who will charge 2 or even 3 percent a year, but you should be able to find a reputable adviser who will take your account for no minimum fee, while charging only the flat 1 percent of market value per year. Whether you make it discretionary or not depends on a variety of factors. The decision need not be made in haste.

diversification
This is the heart and soul of investment strategy. To diversify is to spread the risk by participating in a variety of investment situations. There are five major forms of diversification listed below. But before we get into the subheads, let me add that the really great fortunes in the stock market have been made by concentrating one's assets in one stock. This happens when a man founds his own company, takes a major piece of the stock, and spends his life running that company with great success. Be prepared to put all your eggs in one basket, if you're going to manage the basket. If you're going to let a crowd of strangers carry the baskets, spread the risk!

bond–stock–cash

The most fundamental form of diversification is in spreading your assets between stocks and face-amount holdings such as bonds, savings accounts, and cash. Generally, during inflation such as we're bound to have for the next several years, the less you have in face-amount securities the better. See **cash: reserves** for a discussion of the factors that might have a bearing on your decision as to how much cash you should be holding and in what forms. The bond department of your portfolio should be used for only two things: 1) giving maximum cash income so that the maximum of assets can be devoted to the central problem of preserving your buying power during prolonged inflation; and 2) holding "flower bonds" in case your estate requires such planning. If possible, make your bonds convertible, so that even here you have some degree of protection from the worst long-term effects of inflation.

geographical

When most large companies are either national or international in scope, it seems old-fashioned to think of geographical diversification. But if you like cement stocks, remember that cement is a local product only, and you can buy companies in different areas. The same applies to newspapers, utilities, railroads, airlines, banks, real estate operators, food processors, and mining companies. In gold mining you have the chance to diversify in different countries— South Africa, Canada, Dominican Republic, Australia, and so on. These can be important considerations, especially in gold mining, because gold seems to be a reproach to inflation-minded governments who from time to time attack gold as if *it* were the cause of the great increase in paper money, the consequent rise in prices, and the consequent distress of inflation-ridden people. Geographical diversification is good when you can achieve it without undue compromise of investment potential. But it is a secondary objective in your portfolio. Be aware of its existence and its possibilities, that's all.

industry group

In the stock section of your portfolio, you should try to have something invested in each of the major industry groups or sectors. (This would be especially true when and if we return to normal times, when the money supply is being handled reasonably well and prices are reasonably stable.) It makes sense to divide your stocks fairly equally among the five major sectors: utilities, financial companies, transportation, natural resources, and industrial-commercial companies. This kind of diversification gives your portfolio an ability to ride out the economic cycles more smoothly, because the various sectors have a way of responding at different times and in different ways to the vicissitudes of the economic cycle. There is little evidence that this form of diversification will give you better overall performance throughout a complete cycle, but it will provide you with a more stabilized market value throughout, and that is a very important benefice. For we never know when we shall be required to give an account of ourselves, and it is wise to avoid situations where you might be exposed to the requirement to sell out at the bottom. A diversified portfolio such as this has less pronounced swings in total market value. In normal times the portions should be about equal. With the onset of perpetual and accelerating inflation, the ratio of assets in utilities should be reduced, and the natural-resource sector should be greatly increased. In the mid-1970s, in practice it seems wise to have a token in utilities (and that much only for income) and a token in the financial area, in fast-growing areas such as Florida or Texas; a growth company or two in transportation; up to 20 percent in industry-commerce (depending on your estimate of the business cycle), and fully 50 percent in natural resources, with the emphasis on gold and silver shares.

maturity

You should diversify in the bond section not only among issuers, but also among maturity dates, getting a spectrum of maturities in the future so that you have a regular flow of cash from matured obligations. From time to time this cash can then be used to take advantage of market conditions. This consideration is less important if your bonds are readily marketable before maturity, and if their maturity dates, in any case, are not far away. But you should be aware of this aspect, and even if you buy only a few bonds try to space them at intervals over the next several months or years, according to their maturity dates. (If you have a policy of reinvesting the proceeds in other bonds, then one result is that you'll run your bond portfolio so as to achieve the average interest-rate yield over a period of time.)

number of stocks

You do not have to be a millionaire in order to own enough different stocks to take advantage of the principle of diversification. It has been shown that 95 percent of the benefits of diversifying a stock list can be achieved once you have bought only *ten* different stocks! If you buy more than that, you may have other reasons, such as avoiding taking too large a portion of any one company. If you buy hundreds of different stocks, you simply guarantee that your investment results will be average—no better and no worse than the market averages themselves. You should aim to outperform the averages. One way to do that is to concentrate in a smaller and better-chosen list of companies. Ten different stocks will do very well for anyone with $5,000 or more to invest. Twenty different stocks will keep $1 million very adequately diversified in the market without undue concentration in any given stock. If your broker wants you in and out of thirty different stocks, beware the churner.

timing

I don't mean trying to catch the bottom when buying, or trying to sell at the top. I mean diversifying the times when you do your buying. Suppose you want to buy 200 shares of a stock. It's simple good sense to buy 100 shares now and then wait a while and buy 100 shares later. You can get the average price over that period of time, probably, while guaranteeing that you haven't doubled a mistake. (If the first 100 shares turn out to be real losers, *sell.*) The same principle should apply to establishing your portfolio in the first place. Suppose it is all in cash from an insurance settlement, or all in bonds from your family's estate, or all in cats and dogs from your own manipulations over the years. First get out of the bad investments and into cash. Then set up the list of securities you think you should hold. Establish a schedule for buying these securities over a period of time—perhaps as much as six months, if the amounts involved are fairly substantial. You might make some assumptions concerning our position in the business cycle, the outcome of the next elections, and the outlook for interest rates. Then you would know whether to buy the industrials first and wait for a swing in the natural resource stocks, and so on. In each sector, schedule installment purchases if the sums to be invested warrant it. The whole idea is to avoid going in whole hog the day before some idiot declares war or bankruptcy. The system is a modified version of **dollar-averaging.** It simply gives you diversification in time, just as you have sought diversification in companies and geography. And it all adds up to prudent and accurate portfolio management.

dividend

Cash distributed to shareholders representing their share of
the profits of an enterprise, as decided by the directors (who
usually distribute two-thirds to the stockholders and retain
one-third for further use in the business). The profits are
taxed twice: the corporation pays income taxes, and from
what's left over the corporation pays dividends to the
shareholders, who then pay income taxes on the dividends—
a particularly harsh penalty imposed on those who invest in
American business.

dogs

   See **cats and dogs.**

dollar-averaging

A simple method for beating the averages when you're
establishing a position in a stock. The method requires you
to decide on the total amount of money you intend to put
into the stock: divide that amount into three or four equal
parts. Then use these as installments, and buy your
installments of the stock at regular intervals of time.
Amazingly enough, the result will be that *your* average *cost*
per share will be slightly lower than the *market's* average
price per share during the same period because you will
have bought a few more shares at lower prices than at
higher prices. And this system works the same whether the
market moves up or down during the period when you're
buying. A simple general statement will nail it down.
Suppose you buy at three different times, when the prices
are P, 2P, and 3P. The average price is therefore 2P.
Suppose you invest D dollars in each purchase. Your three
purchases will be D/P shares, D/2P shares, and D/3P
shares, for a total of 11D/6P shares purchased. Your
average price per share will be your total dollars, 3D,
divided by the number of shares you purchased, 11D/6P.

This works out to 18P/11, which is slightly less than the 2P average price per share. The method does not work when you're selling, because there's no way to know in advance whether the market will be going up or down while you're peeling off those installments. So you can't know ahead of time how many dollars to commit to each transaction. What you can do, in selling, is to sell a portion of your holding, and then wait and see what happens. Suppose you had planned to sell in three installments at two-week intervals. You sell the first batch and the market starts rising. *Lengthen the interval between sales* in order to ride a good thing. If you sell the first batch and the market starts falling, do the opposite, and speed up your selling program. This is only an approximate method on the selling side; it depends on feel and luck. But it has been, in my experience, better than the alternatives, which are 1) dumping everything at once, and 2) holding on forever. On the buying side, as the algebra so convincingly demonstrates, dollar-averaging can't miss. But please observe that its benefits are available only if two conditions are *both* present: 1) enough cash in the transactions to make the commission costs reasonable; and 2) enough fluctuation in the stock price to make the exercise worthwhile.

Dow Jones
The great company that publishes *The Wall Street Journal*, *Barron's* magazine, and so on. It also runs a tickertape service carrying business news, and compiles statistics on financial markets—the most famous being the Dow Jones Industrial Averages, a statistical average of thirty major stocks.

Dow Theory

Three generations ago a gentleman named Dow (ancestor of Dow Jones) invented a theory to explain and predict the behavior of stock prices. It involves the Dow Jones Industrials, the Dow Jones Rail Average, and copious infusions of intuition. Probably no more harmful for beating the market than any other system.

E

earned surplus
On the corporate **balance sheet,** earned surplus is the sum
of all after-tax profits not paid out as cash dividends. The
word "surplus" is highly unfortunate; it implies "unnecessary." All it means is "in addition to paid-in capital
contributed by the original venture capitalists."

earnings
In a free market, of course, the name of the game is
earnings. But, strange to say, the concept of earnings is
more easy to define in words than to measure in numbers.
Earnings, or profits, are the normal return on capital (see
interest: originary) plus a special premium that people are
willing to pay for scarce goods. It is this special premium on
scarce goods that attracts capital to newly developing
industries where production can't keep up with demand.
After enough capital has gushed into the industry to build
the factories and install the machines that will meet
demand, the profits of the industry tend to drop: selling
prices are cut, competition becomes intense, weak firms go
under, and the survivors tend to earn a rate of return on
capital that is roughly similar to the rate of return earned
on capital in other mature, stabilized situations—the "originary" return corrected for inflation and risk. Nevertheless,
even if we can't specify earnings to the last penny, we
should make the attempt. Financial analysts look at earnings in many different ways. This helps them to overcome
the problems that arise from the shortcomings of any one
aspect.

after-tax

Almost all corporations are subject to taxes on their earnings. After the taxes have been subtracted from earnings, what's left is after-tax earnings. This is the figure usually reported in news releases. Its principal importance is that this figure determines in the long run the dividend payments declared by the board of directors of the corporation. Over a number of years, the average corporation will pay out about two-thirds of its after-tax earnings in the form of cash dividends to the stockholders. And over a long period of time, the price of the stock will tend to keep a constant relationship to the flow of cash dividends. Obviously, if you can forecast the earnings after taxes, you can forecast the cash dividends, and then the general level of the stock price. However, the after-tax earnings should be corrected for various factors if you want to get a more accurate idea of the long-term dividend-paying power of the corporation. If the earnings include some large lump-sum receipt from a windfall, an insurance settlement, a deferred contribution to a pension fund, sale of assets, or some such one-shot profit, that amount should certainly not be included in any forecast of average future earning power. If the after-tax earnings do not reflect the full corporate tax rate, investigate further; sooner or later the company will have to pay out the full rate, and that means that future pretax profits may *not* flow fully into future dividend-paying ability. After-tax earnings may not only reflect "unreal" profits (such as windfalls or special tax credits), but they may also fail to reflect real expenses, as when a company chooses to call a major new research and development program an "investment" (which does not flow through the income and expense account) rather than an expense (which it most certainly is, in terms of cash). Such "deferred" expenses may become all too real if the program is abandoned or if its prospects suddenly turn sour.

Back in the late 1950s, General Dynamics was reporting nice earnings and paying a cash dividend even while it was spending a couple of hundred million dollars developing a commercial jet transport that had small chance of success. Stockholders who took the earnings at face value and counted on a continuation of the cash dividend were severely shaken when the company finally decided to face the music, **write off** the jet program, and report losses that wiped out the stockholders' equity. The company has made a comeback, but there were many years of struggle. The reported after-tax earnings are only the starting point of any serious investigation of a company's financial strength.

cash flow

Cash earnings or cash-flow earnings are the reported after-tax earnings corrected for any non-cash charges. See also **cash flow.**

deflated

One year a company might report a great improvement in earnings over a previous year. Be sure that the improvement isn't entirely the result of a price rise for the company's products. In times of general price rises, too, be sure that your company's "increases" are greater than those that are attributable to the simple tendency of all numbers to get bigger during a period of monetary inflation. Look underneath the dollar figures and try to find evidence of "real" growth in your company: a higher physical quantity of goods shipped, services performed, and so on. It is not uncommon to find revenue increases arising from price increases that mask a decline in services performed—a situation seen all too often in government-regulated industries.

per share

The earnings (reported, adjusted, cash-flow: whichever you're working with) can be divided by the number of shares outstanding in order to give you the earnings per share. This figure can then be related directly to the price per share on the market. Most of the time, stocks sell between eight and eighteen times the earnings per share. In a period of great enthusiasm, a stock with fabulous prospects may sell for thirty or forty times earnings. The earnings per share are, however, a less reliable basis for measuring stock prices than the cash dividends per share. The reason is that cash dividends tend to be steadier, since they are the result of deliberate policy, while stock prices fluctuate more predictably around the dividend than around the reported or anticipated earnings. The ratio of stock price to earnings per share is called the *earnings multiple*. The better the prospects, the higher the multiple. The higher the multiple, the greater the risk. The ideal: find a company with rosy prospects while the multiple is still low. See also **turnabout.**

pretax

Pretax earnings are useful mainly for analyzing a company's ability to meet interest payments, which come from pretax earnings and are deductible expenses for tax purposes. They should be compared with after-tax earnings to make sure the company is paying something like an ordinary tax rate. Like all earnings, pretax earnings are a "residual" figure— the result of accounting for everything else first, the receipts from sales, the expenditures for necessary items of doing business. What's left over, if anything, is called earnings.

statutory

Regulated industries (electric utilities, railroads, telephone companies, shipping companies, truckers, insurance companies, pipelines, banks, and so on) are required to report their financial results in accord with bookkeeping practices specified by the rate-making authorities. The earnings reported under the accounting rules of the authorities are called statutory earnings and are seldom very useful, because the rate-making authorities are fundamentally political, and their first allegiance is to the political process that keeps them in business. They seek to keep rates low, while explaining to the companies they regulate that the earnings are really satisfactory. The principal method of overstating the statutory earnings is manipulation of the depreciation accounts—stretching the life of the plant and equipment, raising the assumed salvage values in the future, failing to allow for higher replacement costs due to inflation. Sooner or later, however, the regulatory commissions come up against the real world, where "statutory" earnings are ignored and more realistic financial reports are boss. Then, if the regulated company is showing poor earnings and tries to raise new capital, it may find the capital markets closed to it. Then the company must either go back to the regulatory commission for higher rates, or run to the government for "aid." Electric utilities and railroads have reached that point. Airlines are getting there fast—at the speed of the jumbo jet in fact.

unconsolidated

Sometimes a company may own shares in another company. If it doesn't own half, it doesn't add (consolidate) the other company's operations into its own for bookkeeping and reporting purposes. But the other company may have earnings that are significant in the overall picture of the parent company, in which case the investor should know about it. The earnings of the subsidiary company that are attributable to the stock held by the parent company should not be left unconsolidated. They should, instead, be figured out, and some allowance for them made when you evaluate the parent company's stock. The unconsolidated earnings may or may not ever be fully recovered or paid into the parent company, so you shouldn't give them full face value in the market price. But they can be important, as they were for many years in IBM; and you should be aware of them.

economics

Economics is the study of human decision making in an environment of liberty. Its focus is therefore on individual human beings as they make choices. It is the opposite of politics, which is the study of mass decision making in an environment of coercion and compulsion (for the state has the social monopoly on violence). It is therefore a contradiction in terms to speak of the state's having an economic policy. The state has policies, period, which are enforced under the ultimate threat of violence (arrest, imprisonment). Economics can exist only where the threat of violence does *not* exist. When this is understood by the majority of people, the future of liberty will be assured.

education (as investment)

I don't see education in general as an automatically profitable investment. There is such a thing as being overeducated (just as a company can have too much productive capacity). You can be miseducated (just as Ford invested too much in the Edsel). And even if you get the appropriate education, you can take a beating by paying far too much for it. Colleges are probably overcharging by a factor of three or four. You can learn almost anything by sitting in a public library and studying the books. If you need help, an occasional private tutor or an inexpensive course through a correspondence school should do the trick. But blindly pouring money into the hands of the educational bureaucracy can hardly be called an investment. Avoid fads. At one time there was a shortage of engineers. A few years later there was an oversupply of them, and their unemployment rate went up.

eggs
And basket: see **diversification.** Remember, though, that the avenue that has led to the great fortunes has always been concentration.

equity
That amount of a business owned by the shareholders after all debts have been paid off.

estate
What you're worth dead. By the way, it's subject to taxes and administrative expenses. You can escape these by making substantial gifts during your lifetime, if your estate is large enough to justify such activities. The problems begin to run into money when your net worth gets up to $120,000 or so.

exchange rate
The price of one country's currency in terms of a foreign currency.

execution of order
When you ask your broker to buy or sell a security for your account, you're giving him an order to execute. If the stock is listed on an exchange, a simple order to buy will set a long chain of events in motion. You call your broker and ask him to buy X. He calls the order to the order clerk for his firm. The order clerk calls the order to the desk of the *floor partner*—the firm's man on the floor of the exchange. The

floor partner stops by his desk every minute or so and picks up a fresh batch of orders. He takes your order, runs to the place where X is traded, and makes the transaction. He learns the name of the brokerage house that sold you the stock, and he reports the whole transaction back to his order clerk on the floor, who reports to the brokerage firm's order desk, which reports to your account executive, who calls you up and gives you the news. You should squawk if the whole transaction takes too long or is executed at a price too far away from what you had in mind; a reputable broker will try to make adjustments if there's reason to believe something went awry along that complicated chain of communications. But remember: you're a grown-up, and if you say, "Buy at the market," you're not guaranteed any price at all. The broker has his problems too. There are customers who tell the broker to buy stock and don't have the money to pay for it when payment time comes around (four business days later); the broker may have to "swallow" the stock himself. A general rule in getting good executions is to make sure you've told your broker everything he needs to know to do exactly what you want. If you own 100 shares of a stock and want to buy 100 more, tell your broker you want to buy 100 *additional* shares; otherwise he might check your account, see you already have the shares, and fail to take immediate action on the order. If you own 200 shares and want to sell 100, make sure you say you're selling "100 shares out of 200, leaving 100 in the account." That sounds like saying everything twice, and that's what it is. Say it twice, thrice: and get it right the first time. You are dealing in large amounts of money. For any other kind of transaction of similar size you would want a lawyer and an accountant at your elbow. The convenience of dealing by verbal contract is well worth the little extra trouble you may give yourself by going over everything a couple of times.

extractive industries
Companies that mine natural deposits of ore, petroleum, gems, and so on. They're good for long-term resistance to inflation, but bad to the extent that they're subject to sudden political assaults, especially on their depletion allowances, their effect on the landscape, and so on. See also **mining** and **depletion.**

F

face amount certificates

Securities that promise to pay a certain specified sum (the amount printed on the face of the certificate), in currency (dollars), on or before a certain specified date. *No* protection against inflation!

farmland

If you're a farmer, fine. You won't starve. But be prepared to work and to live off your produce, not off the vast fortune to be made in speculative profits from the sale of the farm. Bear in mind, too, that agriculture has been the chief beneficiary of our electricity-and-petroleum civilization. If the ecologists succeed in making it impossible to buy large quantities of energy in those forms, the life of the farmer will be set back one hundred and fifty years. Subsistence level. Think it over.

Federal Open Market Committee

A group in the Federal Reserve System that buys and sells government debt instruments in order to control the money supply. It isn't very successful, because the money supply suffers from jerky movements between very fast rates of growth and periods of no growth at all.

Federal Reserve Board

A group of men who meet regularly to set policy with an eye to controlling the money supply and the general monetary life of the nation. They try to control interest rates, money-supply growth, debt ratios, and so on. And yet, if anything goes awry, they argue that they are powerless and therefore blameless. Which way shall it be?

financial stocks

As a group, the financial stocks offer better-than-average protection against inflation, because they do nothing but manipulate dollar amounts. As inflation proceeds, the number of dollars increases. So, during an inflation, the financial companies are a growth industry. Banks, brokers, insurance brokers, insurance companies, and small loan companies are all in this group. However, they are tightly regulated by state and federal bureaucracies, and that's always a bad situation for the investor-owner. Insurance brokers are probably in the best position to profit from the increased money supply without being too harshly stifled by governmental intervention and regulation.

fixed income

Income guaranteed to remain at a certain level of dollars, such as interest on loans, bonds, notes, savings accounts, and time deposits; payments under annuity contracts, pension payments, retirement benefits; dividends on preferred stock; the "interest component" figured into the total return (or cost) of a "whole" life insurance policy. In all these cases, it is some form of contractual right specified in some fixed and quantifiable number of money units. All's well and good with such arrangements as long as the fundamental factor, the money unit, is relatively stable and reliable. But when it is losing its purchasing power at a rate of 10 percent a year (U.S.) or 25 percent (Great Britain) or a million percent (in class hyperinflations), the contracts themselves lose their value and finally their meaning. Who wants the guaranteed right to receive a bad check? The great feature of common stocks is that they are not fixed claims, but *proportionate*, not only to the profits and cash dividends of a company, but also to the entire net worth of the company. In long-term inflations all dollar numbers tend to rise; so you have a chance (not a certainty, but only a chance) that you'll be able to offset some of the perils of inflation by owning common stocks. As a general rule, in planning your retirement (or indeed your whole financial career) avoid fixed-income contracts as much as possible. If you are forced to accept some form of fixed income (a company retirement and pension plan that you can't reject), then don't fall into the trap of believing you'll be taken care of in old age. Base your plans on the strong possibility that your pension plan won't be worth half what you think it will, and start saving and investing on your own to make sure you have some real buying power when your working days are past. Remember: inflation attacks all contracts. Even if your five hundred dollars a month is guaranteed by every corporation, bank, and insurance company in the country, it's still worth no more than the promises of the politicians, who promise every year to stabilize the dollar but keep on inflating the money supply, thus pulling the rug out from under the buying power of your fixed-income guarantees.

flight from money

In every inflation people begin to fear that prices will not only keep going up, but that they'll rise faster and faster, and that their own incomes won't rise fast enough to keep pace. At this point, they naturally choose to spend their incomes as fast as possible, because the longer they wait the less they'll get for their money. So there is a general "flight" away from money and into tangible goods. Simply to own something solid, people will buy things they don't need, something whose price might rise, rather than something they know is a sure loser, the cash itself. One individual can spend his cash, but a nation as a whole cannot get rid of the cash circulating within its borders. The flight from money therefore results in a greatly increased velocity of circulation. (Toward the end of the 1923 inflation in Germany, when workers were paid twice a day, they ran to the stores to spend their wages before prices doubled again.) The flight from money involves a flight from money instruments, from fixed-income contracts. Bonds are sold because no one wants the guaranteed income. (Bonds, indeed, became completely worthless in Germany and in all other countries that suffered hyperinflation.) It becomes impossible to borrow money at any rate of interest. Capital transactions and capital markets become confused and surrealistic. The end draws near. As an investor you should keep an eye out for signs that a flight from money is starting in this country. Watch out for rising interest rates, a rising velocity of circulation, and a rapidly spreading distrust of the currency, along with the false belief that the higher prices are caused by greedy businessmen. (During the French Revolution, the crowds burned down the bakeries because the price of bread was rising in terms of the worthless *assignat* currency). As a protective measure, you should borrow against your fixed-income contracts, if you have such contracts you can't get rid of. And use the borrowing for speculation in tangible goods or equity claims (stocks, precious metals, coins, and so on). If the inflation continues, every fixed-income contract will become worthless. Prepare now for your own flight from the rotting currency.

floating supply

When a corporation is formed, it sells stock to the public. If it sells a million shares, then a million shares is the amount of stock "issued and outstanding." Theoretically these are the shares that are available for trading back and forth in the financial markets, as people decide to buy or sell. However, it is a mistake to think that the entire issue of outstanding stock is in the floating supply. Large amounts are held in long-term accounts, pension trusts, insurance company portfolios, trust funds, and college endowments.

Many companies have major blocks of stock in the hands of the founding families. In practice the floating supply of stock may be less than half the amount issued. If you are thinking of buying a large block of stock in a company with a small floating supply, be prepared to see the price start rising as soon as your buying power enters the market. And the same is true, of course, on the selling side. This may not apply to the average investor directly, but it does indirectly. You may happen to know of a fine company with bright prospects and a small floating supply of stock. If you *also* know that a large institutional investor is thinking of doing some buying in this stock, you might pick up a few shares ahead of time, "just for the ride." The large buyer will run the price up by 10 percent or more, at which time you can do him a favor and let him have your few shares. Worth trying!

flow of funds
One form of stock-market prediction is based on the flow of funds in a given stock. That's the **volume** multiplied by the price per share. These are, basically, studies of volume, and are particularly useful in giving signals of major turns at tops and bottoms. See also **volume.**

foreign investments
For the average investor, the foreign investment field should be off limits. You can, however, buy shares in domestic companies that operate investment funds concentrating in foreign securities. International Investors runs a portfolio of foreign gold stocks and will some day shift to a diversified position in foreign industrials. On an individual basis, don't get into overseas maneuvers until you have enough money to justify the expense of traveling, lawyers, accountants, custodians, and so on.

formula plans
A formula plan has to do with the **bond ratio** in the
portfolio. A typical plan would require the bond ratio to be
held constant at, say, 40 percent of total market value.
Obviously if the stock market goes up, the bond ratio will
fall, and at a certain point the portfolio manager will sell
stocks and buy bonds in order to keep the ratio constant.
Formula plans force the investor to sell as stocks go up and
buy as they go down. A peculiarity of them is that the
portfolio performance, throughout an entire upward and
downward movement of stock prices, is identical for all
formulas. Variable-ratio formula plans are better.

fractional shares
When a stock splits there are sometimes fractional shares
due. You can take them in cash, or you can add a little cash
by subscription to the company and get an additional whole
share.

G

gambling

What's the difference between investing, trading, speculating, and gambling? You *invest* when you buy a security for the purpose of enjoying the cash income from it in the form of interest or dividends, and when you have no intention of selling it as long as the cash income is maintained. You *trade* when you buy a security for the purpose of selling it at a higher price based on your feeling that it's almost certain to rise. You *speculate* when you buy a security with the intention of selling it at a higher price but without any strong conviction that it's going to go up; you are merely "taking a flier" at it. You *gamble* when you buy a security whose value is certain to go to zero if you're wrong. Note that in investing, trading, and speculating you have something remaining even if you're wrong (assuming you don't wait until the bitter end). In gambling it's all or nothing; if the nag loses, you're dead. Many a trade has turned into an **investment** when the trader has refused to admit failure and has chosen, instead, to consider his stock as a long-term holding. This is typical of amateur portfolio management. When you start a transaction, be very clear in your own mind as to what you expect from it and why you are entering into it. If a trade or a speculation doesn't work out, sell it immediately. But, if an investment turns into a brilliant trade, go ahead and sell it, and place the enlarged proceeds in the kind of investment situation you had in mind in the first place.

For example, suppose you buy 100 shares of a steady company for $100 total, with the intention of receiving the

$6 yearly cash dividend for the rest of your life. Suddenly the stock leaps to $5 a share, and your original investment is now worth $500, although the cash dividend has not changed (perhaps the rise was caused by a merger offer). You would be wise to sell out, pay the capital gains tax of about 25 percent, and reinvest the proceeds—$400 net—in a company like the first one, yielding 6 percent on market price. You would then get $24 a year in cash income (four times what you were willing to settle for in the first place), and there's always the chance that lightning might strike the second investment, too! This kind of maneuver is particularly common when you're trading in convertible securities. You originally purchase a convertible because you find the cash yield satisfactory and are hopeful that lightning might strike the underlying common stock price and give you a nice ride in the convertible. If, shortly thereafter, this happens, then you should enjoy the profits, sell the convertible, and reinvest the proceeds in some other convertible that will give you the proper cash yield. It is, after all, the cash yield on market value that makes the convertible security relatively immune to sudden declines in price. A successful investment may often turn into a short-term trade. Don't try to convert an unsuccessful trade into a long-term investment.

Genstein
Edward Genstein, a physicist by trade, wrote a book that was published and apparently buried in 1954, entitled *Stock Market Profits Without Forecasting*. He described a system that he had used successfully for twenty years and that was confirmed statistically over a period of forty years. It's a system for deciding when to change the bond-stock ratio in your portfolio. It rests on the normal ratio of cash dividends to stock prices; it determines the variation between the current price of stocks and the "normal" price; and it prescribes the bond-stock ratio for the current situation.

How is "normal" determined? By a ten-year moving average. Step #1: find the highest closing price of the Dow Jones Industrial Average in each calendar quarter. Step #2: find the lowest daily closing price for the same period. Step #3: take the arithmetical average of #1 and #2. Step #4: add up the last forty figures in #3. Step #5: divide the figure in #4 by 40. Step #6: find the cash dividends on the Dow Jones Industrial Average for each calendar quarter. Step #7: add up the last forty figures in #6. Step #8: divide the last figure in #7 by 10. Step #9: divide the last figure in #5 by the last figure in #8—this is your current "normal" ratio between cash dividends and stock prices. Step #10: multiply the last figure in #9 by the sum of the last four figures in #6; this gives you the "normal" price of the DJIA based on the most recent full year of dividends. You can now compare the current level of the market with the "normal" level as computed by the Genstein system (which requires nothing more fancy than adding and multiplying). Then you can adjust your portfolio according to a simple schedule:

If the current market level is		*Keep your common stocks to:*
1.45 times normal		10 percent of total market value
1.40		20
1.35		30
1.30		40
1.25		50
.		.
.		.
.		.
1.00		.
.		.
.		.
.		.
normal ./. (divided by	1.25	50
	1.30	60
	1.35	70
	1.40	80
	1.45	90

This may seem cumbersome at first, but the practical working of the system is greatly eased when you learn that you can "play" the ratios by using only a handful of stocks. Genstein discovered that the results are about the same if you simply use a couple of closed-end funds for your common-stock portion: Lehman Corporation and Tri-Continental Corporation. Or you can use any five stocks included in the Dow Jones Industrials and get the same results—say, Union Carbide, du Pont, U.S. Steel, General Electric, Kodak. As for the results: Genstein's work showed that this system would beat the averages in every year going back forty years, and that includes wars, depressions, scares, recessions, assassinations, and all the rest. I know people who have followed this system with satisfactory results. I don't rely exclusively on this, but use it as an independent way to confirm opinions that rest on different sorts of evidence—monetary, political, and "fundamental" analysis (see **security analysis**). The information needed to operate the Genstein system can be obtained from *Barron's* magazine (closing prices, and dividends on the Dow Jones Industrials). As of the summer of 1975 the system found a "normal" value of 1,017.53 for the Dow Jones Industrials and would have signalled a selling point at 1,271.91 (reduce the stock portion to less than 50 percent of total market value) and a buy point of 814.02 (increase the stock portion to more than 50 percent of total market value). The bond portion of the portfolio should, of course, be in money-stable instruments such as savings accounts and short-term notes and bills. I mention this system because it is the most reasonable one I've come across in my career; it has theoretical justification in that the market value of investment securities is closely tied to the long-run level of interest rates; and it works.

gilt-edged securities

Securities of the highest class, having the best credit ratings, the greatest financial soundness, the strongest prospects for continued ability to pay interest and dividends, and the best records of survival during bad times. Long-term government bonds used to qualify as gilt-edged securities, but in times of inflation exactly the opposite is true, and a long-term bond is merely a guarantee of slow but steady financial suffocation. After inflation has really taken hold, there is no such thing as a gilt-edged security any more—hence the widespread feeling of insecurity and confusion, surely one of the great unmeasured costs of inflationary policies.

glamor stocks

Glamor stocks are as hard to define as glamor itself. Look for lots of publicity, little performance, lots of promise, lots of imitators, the appearance of having sprung up from nowhere like a band of mosquitoes. And avoid them, like mosquitoes.

go-go boys

Back in the 1960s a bunch of youngsters from the Harvard Business School and other playpens invaded Wall Street with their computerized forecasts and their pockets full of slide-rules. Everything they touched turned to gold. Lads in their twenties found themselves managing hundreds of millions of dollars of other people's money, people who gladly turned over their money because they had heard that the young men were workers of miracles. What they didn't know was that the great inflation of the Great Society was upon them, and a gorilla flinging spitballs at the stock tables would hit a winner every time. There was the usual myth about eternal prosperity (see **bubble**), and there was the usual greed, with everyone wanting to play the game. And there was the usual aftermath: the go-go boys have gone, their flimsy companies have disappeared in crashes and mergers, and the prudent long-term investor is still doing business in his quiet way. Beware the gentleman who tells you he has the innermost secret of financial success. Ask him how he did during the last recession. Remember: in investing there is no substitute for hard work, patience, and *realistic* objectives. Anyone who would convince you otherwise is a quack, and a dangerous quack. Steer clear!

going public

A privately held company, perhaps with its stock in the hands of one or two families, chooses to issue shares to the general public. There's a moment of enthusiasm surrounding the first public opportunity to inspect the books of account. If you're interested in buying the stock, be patient, and buy it a few months after it has gone public. Usually you can get it 5 or 10 percent below the first issue price.

gold

All the gold that has ever been mined would fit into a small theater. Gold is soft, easy to work, lovely to look at, and indestructible: qualities that have made it a favorite of artisans and jewelers throughout history. It is also easy to assay and subdivide: qualities that have made it useful as money and coin. It is highly reflective, electrically conductive, chemically inert: qualities that make it one of the most useful metals in hypermodern applications from computer circuitry to Apollo re-entry nose-cones. It is distributed widely enough throughout the world so that almost anyone can recognize it, yet its deposits are small enough so that it remains a scarce metal. Small wonder that it has served as money in every civilized country, and small wonder that people are turning to it more and more today, as they see their own money rotting before their eyes. But gold does not earn interest or pay dividends. It requires you to pay for its safekeeping.

bullion

For forty years, following a so-called emergency decree by President Franklin Roosevelt, it was against the law for Americans to own gold in its ingot (bullion) form. But since early 1975, Americans have once again enjoyed that liberty. If you desire to put a portion of your wealth into a compact and easily portable form, which will be anonymous, marketable, impervious to the ravages of inflation, and indestructible, you should take a look at gold bullion. But think twice. At today's prices, the larger ingots cost about fifty thousand dollars apiece. Smaller ingots, cast by commercial smelters and bearing their assay stamp, may not have quite so ready a market. If you wish simply to engage in some in-and-out trading, you'd do better to play the futures markets (see **commodities**)—International Monetary Market, Winnipeg Commodity Exchange, New York Commodity Exchange. Many large banks offer you gold coins and gold bars in sizes from one to four hundred ounces, plus storage services for a fee. But remember: although gold is easy to buy, we haven't had much experience, on this side of the ocean, with the problems of selling gold bars during an emergency in order to raise cash to feed the family, flee the country, or bribe an official to get a relative freed from prison (as happened in Cuba following the Communist takeover).

coins

Gold coins come in two main groups, as do all coins: those of remarkable beauty or rarity (having numismatic value beyond their value as metal), and those without special numismatic value but with a well-defined weight of rare metal in them: these are the so-called bullion coins. Rare coins deserve a place in every large and diversified estate, but they hardly qualify as rainy-day investments. When you want something you can sell to the butcher in return for meat, you mustn't expect the butcher to have a keen appreciation of the value of certain rare coins. You'll take a beating on the trade. But you'll do better if you offer him something he has heard of. A common-date U.S. twenty-dollar gold piece should qualify. It's the most famous U.S. gold coin and it exists in huge quantities. "Hey," the butcher will say, "I've seen those before! They're worth about ten times their face value, aren't they?" So he'll give you credit of $195 or so at his meat market—enough to buy a pound of hamburger or a couple of hotdogs maybe? No—a twenty-dollar gold piece will always buy about two hundred pounds of hamburger, just as one ounce of gold has always bought a good business suit. That's what they mean when they say gold is a "storehouse of value" while paper isn't. So if you're investing in coins, buy the rare dates from a reputable dealer, with good advice. If you're socking a few away for emergency operations (a complete economic fiasco) get common-date U.S. twenty-dollar gold pieces (the "double eagle") and you'll have the most recognizable form of gold money.

mining stocks

Throughout the world and throughout history, gold has been the refuge of financial stability during times of confusion and uncertainty. Thus when the buying power of a currency goes down, people are willing to trade more and more of the rotting currency for an ounce of gold. In different terms, the "price" of gold goes up. One seldom makes a real profit in such situations by trading gold. One simply preserves the buying power of one's assets. But there is a way to make real profits, and that is by investing in gold-mining companies. Obviously if the price of gold rises, the gold mines will enjoy increased income from the same amount of ore processed (assuming they stick with the same grade of ore). If the companies' operating costs climb less rapidly than the price of gold, the profits can expand handsomely. "Operating leverage" begins to assert itself when a small percentage increase in the price of gold leads to a larger percentage increase in the price of gold leads to a larger percentage increase in the operating profits:

Starting price	Later price	Percent change
gold: $200/ounce	$250	+25%
mining cost: $150/ounce	150	—0—
profit: $50/ounce	100	+100%

At the same time there may be an increase in the financial leverage, if people in general begin to assign a higher multiple to the earnings of gold mining companies (see **earnings: multiple**). A stock might initially earn one dollar per share and sell at ten times earnings. After its earnings have doubled, the public may think the stock is a long-term growth company and may be willing to pay fifteen times earnings—in which case the stock will go to 30, or three times its starting price—all on a 25 percent rise in the gold price!

This is the kind of thing that has been possible in gold-mining shares since I first recommended them in a book published in 1968 *(Death of the Dollar)*. I am asked if "the bloom is off the rose" now. The answer is a loud and definite No. As long as the government insists on destroying the purchasing power of the dollar, the dollar price of gold will rise. And if history is our teacher, we have learned that the rise will be faster and faster until the whole process falls apart in a hysterical lunge toward order, any kind of order, to stop the madness. So, yes, buy gold stocks. Buy a few issues in the Western Hemisphere (American and Canadian companies: Homestake, Rosario, Campbell Red Lake) and a few South Africans (Amgold, Free State Geduld, Kloof, Western Holdings, Vaal Reefs). Pay particular attention to Amgold (Anglo American Gold Investment Ltd.), because it's a holding company with interests in a couple of dozen

operating gold mines, and that one issue all by itself gives
you wonderful diversification.

How much of your portfolio should you put into gold-
mining shares now? Well, back in 1969 I established a
policy of adding 10 percent of all portfolio values to the
gold-mining shares for each year of the 1970s. By 1972 the
portfolios I was managing were 20 percent in gold. By 1975
they were about 50 percent in gold and silver. By the end of
1976 they should be about 70 percent in precious metals—
stocks, bullion, coins. These, I must emphasize, are individual portfolios, where I know the investors and can assess
their ability to handle the risks that arise from a certain lack
of balance in a portfolio (when you're 70 percent in
anything, you're out of balance). I think almost everyone
should protect himself from inflation, and I think gold-
mining shares are an excellent way of doing that; but I
hesitate to recommend a heavy concentration on gold in
any portfolio I don't know individually. A certain drug may
work wonders, but no doctor would prescribe it for the
whole population. Like medicine, investment advice is best
practiced on an individual footing.

good-the-week
Like a **day order,** except that it's valid for the week.

good till canceled (GTC)
Like a **day order,** except that it's valid until the customer
cancels it. Watch out for such orders. Keep a record of their
existence. You can easily get snarled in paperwork.

government intervention
It seems to be a general rule that all government intervention in free markets is "counterproductive"—i.e., the intervention leaves things worse than they would have been
otherwise. The theoretical and general reason for this is that
political decisions are necessarily made in the absence of

real market prices; so there is no way to determine, by a political process, what would be the most efficient use of capital. From the standpoint of the investor, it is enough to know that the best long-term investments are in companies that are as far away as possible from the arbitrary world of political decision making.

government regulation
Almost every line of business is now regulated by government. In seemingly unregulated businesses, the effect of the tax law is highly directive in itself. The general rule in investing is to avoid the most regulated industries, mainly because of the governmental prejudice against profits.

grandfather dollars
No, I don't mean your inheritance. I mean the dollars held by a man when he's young. In normal times an investment should throw off cash income and also accumulate in market value through the internal reinvestment of earnings. In normal times you might expect an investment to double in fifteen or twenty years, and to double again in another fifteen or twenty years. The money saved and invested today is the grandfather of the money represented by the market value thirty or forty years down the road. So the young man might do well to understand that a dollar saved and invested in his youth may mean many dollars of market value later on. But—who can save at a time like that? Life, as President Kennedy was fond of saying, isn't fair.

graph
A plotting of stock price changes against time intervals. Always misnamed "chart" on Wall Street. See also **chart** and **random walk.**

Greater Fool Theory
The reigning wisdom during speculative bubbles. No attempt is made to measure stock prices against an external
standard. If some fool bought the stock for 90 yesterday and
I bought it for 100 today, there'll be an even greater fool I
can sell to tomorrow at 110, right? Wrong.

Gross National Product (GNP)
A government statistic that tries to give a dollar figure to
the sum total of goods and services produced in the U.S.
Unfortunately it includes "services" that no one would pay
for if he had his choice (the federal budget, for one thing),
and "services" such as the rental value of the homes we
occupy and own. The GNP is a nice big round number, but
it's not accurate within 50 percent.

growth
During normal times the investor is satisfied with the
interest return on his capital. During inflationary times he
must look for something more, and its name is growth. He
shoots for growing cash dividends, which come from
growing earnings, which in turn come from growing sales
and revenues. Most investors, then, are looking for long-
term growth, but very few of them seem to understand that
the only truly fundamental long-term growth is population
growth. All other forms of growth are temporary: a fad will
start at zero and **top out** when it serves 10 percent of the
population, at which point its growth rate drops to that of
the population itself; a technical innovation will take over a
sector of the population by replacing its inferior pre-
decessors, only to be replaced in turn by an even better
invention; and so on. It is obvious that the growth we are
looking for is growth at a faster rate than the long-term
growth rate of the population. But it is equally obvious that
no company can keep that up forever; sooner or later it

would cover the entire market, the entire national economy, and then there would be no further room for growth (the same could apply on a global scale). So we are looking for the growth *phase* of products, companies, and industries. See also **cycle.**

company

A growth company is one that has shown an ability to grow (in revenues, sales, and profits) faster than the national economy, and has maintained this growth through a couple of years when most companies were having trouble breaking even. Of course every company starts small, with no record of achievement, no profits, and management untested in the storms of the marketplace. Every new venture is a growth speculation by definition. But 95 percent of all new ventures fail. Until you've acquired a great deal of experience in picking investments, don't invest in brand new companies. Such investments are mere ventures, with no calculable prospect of paying dividends or returning your capital. Pick companies that have at least $75 million in annual sales revenues. That's big enough to have been around for a while, to have survived the first crucial years when most companies go broke (most of the failures of new ventures occur in the first two years; a company that's five years old has a tremendous chance of staying in business if it has begun to show a profit by then). It's big enough to command attention from banks and other lending institutions (which often provide, in addition, good advice to management); to assure a ready market for the stock, listing on an exchange, daily quotation in the newspapers, and news coverage of corporate developments. Don't call it growth unless the rate is at least twice the national average. And don't call it a *rate* of growth unless you see it sustained for at least three years, preferably five!

cycle

The typical company that starts from zero and launches an established business grows at a terrific rate for the first several years. It is not unusual to see sales doubling every year for a few years; then watch the growth rate slow down to 50 percent a year, then to 15 percent (a rate that is often sustained for decades), then to something on a par with the national economy's growth rate. This is the *standard growth curve* of the successful corporation. The big money is not made at the end, when the company is plodding along with the population increase; nor is it made at the very beginning, because there isn't room for big money in a small venture, and usually the entrance price is high in comparison with the profits of the first year or so. The big money is made when you buy into a company that has established itself somewhere between the 50 percent and the 15 percent growth rate; and when you hold for years, for decades, as long as that growth continues. An investment that grows 15 percent a year will double in five years. Hold it for thirty years and you'll wind up with sixty-four times your starting capital! So—try to keep your investment diversified in different companies, but try to make all those companies qualify in the long-term growth category. Get in early in the growth cycle after the company has settled down for the long pull. Then stay for the big payoff.

industry

If an innovative company is truly successful, it may attract a band of imitators, as happened in the computer business. Then you have a growth industry, that is, a group of companies, all concentrating on one field, whose total sales are growing at a rate several times that of the national economy. Watch out for companies of secondary importance in growth industries. Remember the growth cycle. When the initial phase has worn off, there will be price competition, mergers, dropouts. Almost 2,500 automobile companies were started in this country, including the Rickenbacker Motor Car Company. Only a handful survived the competition that set in during the 1920s when the industry was settling down for the long haul. Find the industry leader and stay with it. The leader is the company with the best research, the highest proportion of current sales produced by new products (any way you measure "new"—introduced in the last five years, the last three, the last two), the largest and strongest position in patents, the strongest cash position, the least debt, the highest profit margin on operations (this last may be the most important, because when the price-cutting starts, the high-profit producer is the last to stay in the game). A growth industry is not an industry populated by growth stocks. It's an industry that's on its way toward consolidation, an industry with a large number of companies (only a few of which will survive into full maturity). When every stock in an industry is accorded a high **earnings multiple,** you are in the presence of a **bubble.** Watch out. If you can't clearly identify the industry leader, stand aside until the crowd has thinned out a bit. It will, sooner than you think; and then you can calmly buy the best in the business.

nominal

Nominal growth occurs when a company does not expand its physical production of goods or services but does report an increase in dollar value of sales or profits. This can occur when the company raises its prices; and that, in turn, can occur in a single company or industry (when, for example, the price of gold rises, the gold mines earn more money), or throughout an inflationary economy. Nominal growth is the opposite of **real growth.**

portfolio

A growth portfolio is a selection of different stocks in different industries, whose common characteristic is that they are growing, in real terms, at rates at least twice the rate of the national economy, the population, or some other broad measurement.

real

Real growth is any increase in the physical volume of goods or services sold. Opposed to **nominal.**

stock

A growth stock is the common stock of a **growth company.** Don't pay too much for growth. A rough rule for evaluating the market price of a growth stock is this: its **earnings multiple** should have the same relation to its growth rate as the average stock's earnings ratio has to the average stock's growth rate. Example: say the Dow Jones Industrials are growing (in revenues, profits, combined, on average, over a couple of years) at 5 percent a year and selling at twelve times current earnings. You are looking at a growth company that's growing at 15 percent a year, and its stock is selling for twenty-four times current earnings. Should you buy that stock? Well, the company is growing at three times the average rate, and if its stock were selling at three times the average price it would be at thirty-six times current earnings. So, at twenty-four times earnings, it could be bought for the possibility of a short-term rise; and it certainly could be bought and held on a long-term basis for capital appreciation.

What *is* long-term? The tax law says six months, but the investor and the investment analyst think in terms of three or four years. Preferably five, if you can see that far ahead. It's amazing what a small amount of growth will do. Suppose you find a company that looks as if it will grow at

15 percent a year for a few years. You buy the stock at twenty-four times earnings, thinking it should really be worth thirty-six times earnings. You turn out to be mistaken: the company grows at 15 percent for the next three years and then, due to premature aging, slows down to a growth rate of 10 percent. If the earnings multiple drops to twelve times, your market value will be the same (in nominal terms) as when you started. And, if the company's growth has slowed, we can assume that the management will be less interested in reinvesting the profits, and will instead pay a larger portion of the profits in cash dividends. If it started by paying 10 percent of the profits in cash and gradually increased that ratio to 60 percent in the sixth year (after three years of 15 percent growth and three more years of 10 percent growth), then the cash yield in the sixth year would be 5.04 percent based on your original cost. And presumably that ratio, or **yield** on original cost, would keep growing at 10 percent a year. So—even assuming you made a serious mistake in your original projections—you have been "saved" to a great extent by the growth that did occur. No wonder the investment analyst looks for growth. You should, too.

gunslingers
The **go-go boys.** A couple of bad years separated them from the men.

H

haste

The cradle of catastrophe. In the investment business, all the great mistakes are made in a hurry. Don't ever let anyone hustle you into a decision!

hedge

A maneuver to avoid risk. It involves being **long** and **short** at the same time in substantially the same items. The main economic use of hedging is in manufacturing operations. Suppose you produce silver necklaces and you sign a contract in January to deliver $50,000 worth to the purchaser (a chain store) in June. You don't have the silver on hand, but you expect to buy it before June. You are technically "short" silver, because you have contracted to deliver something that you don't own. You stand a great risk of losing money if the market price of silver rises. You can neutralize that risk entirely by buying the silver now, but that would tie up your capital for a few months and would cost you storage and insurance charges to boot. So you buy a silver futures contract (see **commodities**) calling for delivery to you of the silver you need at a future date and at a guaranteed price. You're covered. You have "hedged yourself" in the futures market.

You can hedge in securities also. When a company has common stock as well as a bond or a preferred stock that is convertible into the common, it's sometimes possible to sell the stock short and go long the bond (or vice versa) and make a little money no matter which way the ball bounces. Don't try these high-wire acts, however, until you have learned to walk securely on the good solid earth of investment management.

hidden problems

Financial statements seem to disclose a great deal of information, but there are great gaps you should know about. The real value of plant and equipment is always subject to debate. Whether "goodwill" is an asset that should be counted in the millions is another good question. Inventory of goods in process may look fine, but is there a real assurance that the values given on the balance sheet can be "realized" by sale in the markets? Research and development expenditures can be added to the book value of goods in process; but sooner or later they'll have to be run through the expense accounts. Long-term debt may not describe the whole picture: the company may have signed a bunch of long-term lease agreements, too, which constitute just as firm a claim on future income as interest payments. Unfunded pension liabilities should be considered. Income statements that benefit from deferred contributions to pension funds should be adjusted. The financial statements say nothing at all about the health and happiness of the key men who make the whole thing possible. They say nothing about the possibility of government intervention and regulation. "Cash and equivalent" may include short-term investments that may or may not be worthwhile; when Penn Central went broke, many other companies found themselves taking large losses on their short-term loans to that huge and hapless giant. Those loans had been accounted for on the other companies' books as short-term investments that were considered to be as good as gold.

hidden values

Financial statements can carry or conceal values as well as problems. A railroad may carry its land at low values on the books of account, even though the land may include hundreds of thousands of acres in or near major oil fields. There may be valuable timber on it. A publishing company may own thousands of acres of timberland. A research outfit may be halfway through developing a major new gizmo. Another company may have written off its expenses years ago on a product that will be introduced next year (typical of pharmaceutical manufacturers), and it should all be gravy. A company's leases may run fifty years at a flat rate, constituting a tremendous and growing "profit" in times of inflation. Investments carried on the books at cost may have a market value several times higher. A new management team may be about to break into the board room. A competitor's major new product may be about to collapse because consumers have rejected it, leaving the field to our heroes. Unconsolidated subsidiaries may be prospering. The general idea is this: don't let your study of a company stop with the financial reports. There's a lot going on in other fields, and the more you know, the better.

historical cost

The number of dollars spent, at the time, to acquire an asset. See also **depreciation.**

holding company

A company whose business it is to manage its own investment portfolio, which it "holds" for the benefit of the people who own the holding company's shares. Contrasted with operating company.

home

Rent your house or own it? See **car**. The same equation applies to all forms of rentals. You have to do some very sharp figuring to come out ahead, one way or another. Here are some typical numbers. Let's say you buy a house, putting down $10,000 in cash and taking out a mortgage of $30,000 to be paid off in twenty years with 9 percent interest. Maintenance on the house starts at $1,500 a year, and because of inflation it grows at 7 percent a year. Taxes start at $2,000 a year and also grow at the inflationary rate of 7 percent. Interest starts at $2,700 a year but drops to zero at the end, averaging about $1,400 a year. Let's assume, in a 30 percent tax bracket, that taxes and interest are deductible, so the operating expense of the house is reduced by 30 percent of $5,400, or $1,620. The net after-tax cost of running the house over a twenty-year period averages $6,780 a year, with prices rising at a steady rate of 7 percent a year.

Consider the alternative of renting an apartment. You put the $10,000 you would have used as a down payment into a securities portfolio. Add to it the $1,500 a year that you would have been "saving" by paying off the mortgage—on average, the equivalent of $15,000 for a twenty-year period. The average paid-in cost of the portfolio is therefore $25,000. There are no expenses. Instead you have income—at the rate of 5 percent to start with, but growing at 7 percent, and averaging $5,000 a year. Thirty percent of the dividend is paid in taxes, leaving net investment income of $3,500 a year. Starting with an apartment rental of $5,000 a year with increases of 7 percent a year; the average rent for the period is $10,000 a year. Your net cost after taxes is therefore $10,000 minus $3,500, or $6,500 a year. The figures are very close: $6,780 a year to own a house, $6,500 a year to rent an apartment and invest the difference in cash outgo.

What happens over the twenty years to the equity values of the house and the portfolio? If prices rise at 7 percent, the $40,000 house will rise in market price to $160,000; the mortgage will be fully paid off, so the owner will have an equity of $160,000 to show for his pains (plus twenty years of mowing the grass). Meanwhile, the apartment owner's portfolio has been invested with great attention to long-term growth in excess of the inflation rate; it is not at all unreasonable to look for, and achieve, 10 percent capital appreciation over a long period of years. The apartment dweller's initial $10,000 plus the $1,500 yearly additions invested at 10 percent for twenty years will grow to exactly $168,187—almost exactly equal to the equity of the house-owner. So it's basically a matter of taste. The market functions to equalize the interest rates in all forms of investment. If you can rent more cheaply and invest faster, you're better off to rent. If you can find a great house for a small price and a mortgage at 2 percent, buy it. Just remember that the arithmetic isn't overpowering. The deciding factor is how you want to live. And if the deciding factor happens to have gracious ways and a pretty smile, your financial adviser will go along with whatever you decide.

home (as an investment)
See **real estate.** Basically I don't like using the home as an investment because it's too hard to separate its dwelling value from its investment value. And if you can't be precise about the investment value, how can you measure the investment yield?

home-improvement loans
The same financial principles are at work in the question of home-improvement loans: interest rates versus portfolio appreciation rates. There is the additional question of the outlook for the neighborhood. I take it for granted that you

bought the house in the first place because you thought the neighborhood would do no worse than any other neighborhood in maintaining the market value of its real estate. Now you have lived there a few years and have a choice between 1) moving, 2) improving or expanding the house, and 3) staying put and making do. The decision must rest on factors other than financial (see the discussion under **home**). The choice rests on the outlook for your own specific neighborhood and whatever alternative neighborhood you may have in mind. No general statement can apply to such questions. Anyone who thinks he can give you advice on that kind of question is a crank. If you like your neighborhood, think it's worth investing in, and have a choice between borrowing to make the improvement or putting your own cash into the house, you can make the financial decision on the basis of the discussion already given. The same goes for co-ops and condominiums.

hot issues
If your broker calls you up and says he has a hot issue, ignore him. There *are* hot issues like new issues of stock that are almost guaranteed to have a quick rise in price, but the chances are strongly against your ever seeing them. If you do get one, and then you want to sell and nail down that quick profit, your broker will frown and say he'd been under the impression you were investing for the long pull. But that's inconsistent: if it was long term, why the salivation over the hot-issue aspects?

hyperinflation
See **inflation.**

hypothecation

Putting property into the hands of others as a guarantee of your performance under a borrowing agreement. If you don't pay off, the lender can sell your property to satisfy his claim. Collateralization.

I

income

See also **capital.** Many investors make an unnecessarily rigid
distinction between income and capital. It is like trying to
distinguish some fundamental aspects in water that falls
from the faucet and water that collects in the bowl. Income
is capital flowing. Capital is income saved. In normal times
it's a good general rule to avoid spending capital and to
spend only income. In inflationary times you may find it
necessary to spend far less than your investment income
and to reinvest a portion of the income in order to hold
your position in terms of the buying power of your capital.
A paradox: If you invest for maximum current income in
inflationary times, you run the risk of losing your buying
power over the long run; whereas if you invest for
maximum long-term growth of capital values, you stand the
best chance of enjoying a constant buying-power income
over the years to come. Growing companies tend to pay out
less in cash dividends (see **growth**) and reinvest the retained
earnings in their own profitable operations; they do the
saving and reinvesting *for* you out of the current income
flows that your shares represent. The beginning of financial
wisdom is to remember that income is capital in a different
form, and that capital is income in a different form. There
are times when you may safely spend more than your
income, and times when you must save as much income as
you can. Be aware of the times and what they require; be
flexible.

income statement
An account of receipts and expenditures over a given period of time. Look for receipts that don't mean cash, and that aren't normal and recurring, expenses that aren't cash and that are deferred (to pretty up the current figures), and for taxes that don't reflect the full tax rates.

index (stock prices)
There are various indices of stock prices. The Dow Jones Industrial Average (DJIA) is the most famous and has the longest historical background. Standard & Poor has several broadly based stock market averages. *The New York Times* publishes its own stock averages. The New York Stock Exchange and the American Stock Exchange publish indexes of their listed stocks. The over-the-counter market publishes a stock index. At times the indices will conflict with each other as a result of differences in their elements. By and large they move together, accurate to within 10 percent or so of each other's readings. This is one reason why prediction systems based on trivial moves in one index can be considered unreliable. The indices themselves aren't that accurate.

indicators
Many years ago, the National Bureau of Economic Research developed three sets of economic statistics that provide information on the phase of the economic cycle. These are the so-called leading, coincident, and lagging indicators. The illustration shows that the leading indicators usually turn down several months before the economy enters into a recessionary phase and turn up some months before the bottom has been reached. A very useful set of statistics, available in major financial publications.

PERCENTAGE OF INDICATORS EXPANDING

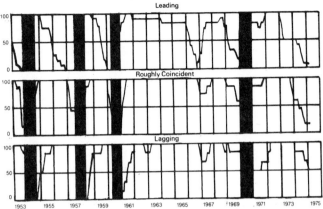

industrials

This is not an analysis of industries. Instead, I simply want to introduce you to the great variety of industrial stocks available, and to give you my own recommendation in each industrial category. Caution: the recommendation is made on the basis of the fundamental economic trends visible in the industry at the time I'm writing; don't take action yourself until you have checked the newest developments within the industry and the relative movements of stock prices. It may be that an industry has favorable prospects but that every stock in the industry is selling for 100 times earnings. In that case, you've missed the boat, and you'll have to look elsewhere.

aerospace (defense)

Outside the economic cycle entirely; dependent on government contracts; low profits subject to renegotiation; should be bought when everyone is convinced we'll never have another war and sold for trading profits. Don't use these as long-term holdings. Dividends are not secure.

air freight

A growth industry; long-term outlook highly favorable; no high-yielding stocks available, but as earnings grow, yields keep increasing. Industry has certain contracyclical aspects.

air transport

Not recommended until situation with government regulation is cleared up. With reduced regulation, reduced fares, and reduced overlapping of routes, industry could prosper mightily; no promise of that as long as government insists on arbitrary regulation, and industry management is afraid to disagree.

aluminum

A generation ago, a growth industry. Now humdrum, high-cost, cyclical. Not recommended.

atomic energy

Worth watching now. Sooner or later this will, shall we say, mushroom into a growth industry. When the time is ripe, a few judicious selections should work wonders in your portfolio. Perhaps uranium mining would be the way to play it. Note the uranium interest of some gold-mining companies.

automobile

Not a growth industry, but highly attractive for trading in and out. GM, for example, has gone from 90 to 31 in the last couple of years and is now on its way back to 90. And when it hits 90, it will be on its way back to 31 again. Nothing nicer than the chance to go short-terming in the world's largest and richest manufacturing corporation!

auto parts

Original-equipment people have the same problems as auto makers, but more so. Replacement parts, so-called after-market, a stabilized business without great attraction.

auto trucks

Not recommended. Supplier to the trucking industry, which has more problems than anyone needs.

beverages

Brewers are local, stabilized, with some chance for seasonal trading, not attractive for long haul. *Distillers* have too many problems and poor management; stay clear. *Soft drinks* offer good chances for long-term growth; try to buy the majors when they're selling cheap.

building materials

Great industry for short-term trading based on cycles in the building business, but you need second sight and the nimbleness of the panther. Major influences are politics, interest rates, politics, labor unions, politics, business conditions, and politics. Expert preparation recommended.

chemicals

Average prospects, cyclical. Ho-hum.

coal

With some utilities shifting to coal, the outlook over the next five or ten years is quite favorable for the major soft-coal companies, and for the railroads that do the hauling.

confectionery

No great attraction here.

conglomerates
Definitely not. See **conglomerates.**

containers
Average prospects for all parts of the industry—metal, glass, paper. Not very good as trading vehicles either.

copper
Cyclical, subject to extreme political risks, highly dependent on market price, which jumps up and down like Mexican bean. Great for trading, but not for long-term investment.

cosmetics
Signs of growth here, but problems with fad and fashion. Large, diversified companies offer the best protection from risk of instant obsolescence of product.

drugs
A great industry. Buy two or three different companies to make sure you'll hit a few winners from the research labs. Wait until some politician announces he's going to investigate the industry. Then the stocks will fall and you can buy them cheap.

electrical equipment
Major manufacturers of the heavy stuff: about the same story as the auto makers, and take her from there. Household appliances: not attractive. Electronics: buy a good Japanese stock.

fertilizers
If the politicians would leave agriculture to the free market, there would be a growth demand for fertilizers. The industry is worth watching. One of these days it could sprout like Indiana corn.

finance companies

Large equipment-leasing companies offer better-than-average prospects during an inflation. Small-loan companies run the risk of bad debts in hard times. Stay away from the smalls. Among the bigs, look for extremely strong financial position above any other criterion. It may be needed.

food

Canned foods have average prospects. *Dairy products* are perhaps slightly better than average, enjoying good solid sales curves (recession resistant?). *Meat packers* have low margins, tough costs, average prospects, and are not for the investor. *Packaged foods* should show good growth in "convenience foods," if you can find stocks at reasonable prices.

forest products

Timberlands, yes; sawmills, no.

gold mining

Superb. The best long-term holdings of the 1960s and 1970s, and if the politicians keep gutting the currency, the gold shares will be the best holdings of the 1980s as well. See **gold.**

home furnishings

So-so.

hospital supplies

Good growth here, with some problems in profit margins. One or two of the biggest companies might qualify as long-term holdings if you can get them at decent prices.

hotels and motels
Tough analytical problems, separating leisure travel from business travel from real-estate speculation. Problems with finance and management. Avoid.

lead and zinc
Prospects better than average, especially if there's a good hunk of silver in the ore. Cyclical. Buy before boom.

leisure time
Pretty good prospects! Absence of government regulation; broad markets; good margins in new items. With forty million people receiving government payments, there's a lot of leisure out there for the working man to sell to!

machine tools
The greatest boom-and-bust industry of them all. Use strictly for trading on the business cycle.

machinery
Agricultural: cyclical, but with strong underlying growth in the long-term future. *Materials handling:* better than average, but with sharp ups and downs. *Industrial:* average too shaky. *Oil well:* looking better all the time, prospects above average.

metal fabricating
Not particularly attractive.

mobile homes
Looks as if they've shot their wad.

motion pictures

The industry is recovering from the long decline that set in when the government intervened in the distribution-exhibition process. Even when a company prospers, not much seems to filter down to the public stockholder. Not for the prudent or cautious investor.

office equipment

Growth prospects between good and super. The best in the business is IBM, which the government keeps trying to break up into little pieces. Wait until the Justice Department attacks, then buy the stock cheap.

offshore drilling

Not so simple as it looks. But the major companies do have promising outlooks for the next ten years or so. Some interesting **convertibles** in this field.

oil

The industry has been under heavy siege by the government, but it will continue to operate, if for no other reason than that several hundred million people enjoy using its products. Major crude producers and international operators look good for the long-term holder. Good dividends too.

paper

Sorry, but I'd rather have the timberlands. For some reason the paper industry never seems to live up to its promises.

pollution control

A typical fad. Five years from now no one will remember it. Don't be stung in a good cause.

publishing
The big companies, with diversified operations in textbooks, trade books, and related items, are worth including in any conservative long-term portfolio. Growth rate should remain modestly above average.

radio and television broadcasting
As long as the industry is controlled by the government, long-term prospects are unclear. Industry has undeniable growth features but their attractiveness is outweighed by the irrational factors resulting from political intervention.

railroad equipment
To be traded on a cyclical basis, although the larger firms have long-term growth possibilities.

real estate trusts
Forget it. You're better off buying raw acreage.

restaurants
Too faddy. If you're lucky and get in on the ground floor of a fast-growing new chain, fine. But there's not a good investment-type stock in the group.

retail stores
Slow death.

savings and loans
Unsound loan portfolios, "backed" by unfunded insurance agencies, equals dubious investment. Touch not.

shoes
No.

soap
The big ones are pretty strong, relatively free of government intervention, and deeply imbedded in their markets. Growth better than average. With strong finances and a good dividend, some of these stocks qualify for long-term holding.

steel
Same as the auto makers. Play them for trading in and out of the economic cycle.

sugar-beet refiners
Market is distorted by government interference. If the industry were allowed to function freely, it might offer some wonderful investment opportunities.

textiles
Apparel manufacturers: thin margins, occasional problems, but good long-term prospects, especially in denims. *Synthetic fibers:* no real high-quality companies. *Textile products:* only average appeal.

tires and rubber goods
Prospects are only average. Don't go out of your way for these stocks.

tobacco
Cigarette makers offer long-term growth at a very unrewarding rate. Snuff, in fact, looks much better.

toys
Can be good, but depends too much on luck.

truckers
Too much governmental regulation.

vending and food service
Average prospects.

inflation

Any increase in the money supply. It *causes* a general rise
in prices, relative to the price level that would exist if the
money supply were constant. *Creeping* inflation is money
growth at a rate that doesn't require major changes in your
financial planning. *Suppressed* inflation occurs when the
money supply increases, but the government outlaws rising
prices and forbids you to export your accumulating cash.
Cash balances in the banks rise to crazy heights. *Runaway*
inflation occurs when the government no longer makes any
effort to slow the money growth. *Hyperinflation* occurs
when the people, in panic, attempt to reduce their cash
balances to zero, and the inflation rate moves into astronomical figures. When it takes several billion dollars to mail
a letter, we'll be in the hyperinflationary phase of our long
inflationary spree.

inheritance

The most important thing about the possibility of inheriting
something is that you know enough about it ahead of time
to coordinate your financial planning with the facts. If
you're going to inherit a portfolio of tax-exempt bonds, or a
hundred acres of Maine, or a small trust fund devoted
entirely to gold shares, you should know about it *now.* Then
you can set up a program to cover the entire family
financial picture. Do everything you can to avoid trusts. If
you can't avoid them, try to get wise family members
appointed as trustees. Never a bank! See also **windfall.**

inside information
Anything known by the officers or employees of a company and not by the general public. Government regulations make it pretty hard for the insiders to profit from their information, but the general public is still permitted to act in its own interest on the basis of special knowledge. It's harder than you might think to make money on the basis of inside tips. The trickiest thing is figuring out whether the price of the stock hasn't *already* discounted the insider's "news." The safest way to play inside information is to assume that the whole world knows it. Then it becomes straightforward, uncomplicated *information,* and that's what you want anyway. Don't load it up with any special significance.

insider
An officer or director of a company. Insiders' transactions in their own companies' securities are reported to the SEC and made public, but they don't consistently reveal anything. There are reasons to buy and sell other than one's opinion of the outlook for a given security. Hence any trading system based on "insiders' reports" is not on firm ground.

insurance
Insurance is the least understood aspect of family finance. Yet it need not be, for the concepts underlying an insurance contract are simple enough. Insurance is a financial offset to misfortune. If you already possess enough financial strength to withstand the misfortune, you don't need to buy insurance from anyone else; you are "self-insured." It is always preferable to be self-insured. You maintain control of the assets devoted to the insurance function, and you save money three ways: 1) you don't pay a commission, because there isn't any salesman; 2) you don't pay a

management fee, because there's no company being hired; 3) you earn a higher rate of return on your own assets than government commissions permit insurance companies to earn.

Nevertheless, if you buy an insurance contract, it works on the "law of large numbers." Suppose we are talking about Misfortune "A." In any group of one thousand citizens, this misfortune will strike five citizens in any given year. (Records going back a century show that the average has always been five; in some years six, in some years four, but five on the average.) Misfortune "A" is considered to require a financial offset of $1,000, because that's what people ask for, on average, when they're hit by this particular problem. The situation is commercially insurable. A company could sell a contract to each of the thousand members of this group. In doing so, the company would expose itself to a statistical certainty of having to pay compensation under five contracts. Five times $1,000 is $5,000—the amount of "risk" the company shoulders for the thousand worriers. If the company can collect $5.00 from each member of the group, its risk will be "covered." In practice there will be additional costs—sales commissions, management fees, and a slight extra charge that compensates the company for the slight extra risk it assumes (the risk that this will be an unusual year and seven cases of Misfortune "A" will be reported). In practice, also, there will be a slight reduction of the fee, thanks to the company's investment income. For it receives its $5,000 "up front"—at the beginning of the year and pays out the $5,000 in claims at some later time. It may have the use of the $5,000 for six months or more. And it can earn interest and dividend income on that money, and apply some portion of that investment income to reducing the cost of the insurance contract to the buyer.

Please note that almost all forms of insurance contract speak in terms of a fixed number of dollars. They are *face-*

amount contracts, like a bond or a savings account. During times of rapid inflation, any long-term contract for a fixed amount of currency is certain to suffer great loss in buying power; to the extent that the contract is truly insurance, you are progressively underinsured as inflation undercuts the real value of the offset you expect to receive for Misfortune "A." Look at the investment portfolio of the average insurance company. See how much of it is in bonds, losing 8 to 10 percent of their buying power per year. That's a gigantic hidden cost of commercial insurance during an inflationary epoch.

accident

Collision insurance is most effective when it is not a hidden form of savings account but genuine insurance. You should insure against misfortunes, not the ordinary scrapes and mishaps of life. This means that you should only buy insurance against major disasters, and self-insure against the minor ones. The "deductible" amount should be as high as you can handle. A few representative numbers will make the point. In my neck of the woods, a $50-deductible collision policy for my particular car, for one year, requires a premium of $130. A $100-deductible policy costs $100. A $250-deductible policy costs $60. Assuming you can earn 10 percent on your money, here's how the arithmetic pans out:

INSURANCE POLICY

	$50 deductible	*$100 deductible*	*$250 deductible*
Invest @ 10%	$ 50	$100	$250
Pay premium	130	100	60
Total cash up front	180	200	310
At end of year:			
Reward (no accident)	55	110	275
Risk (accident)	175	190	285
Reward/risk ratio	31.4%	57.9%	96.5%

Those numbers assume that if you insure yourself to the extent of $50, you add that immediately to your investment portfolio, which earns 10 percent a year. And you will observe various other assumptions that don't really change the substance of the reasoning. The more you self-insure, the more money you save. Note also the reward/risk ratio. It climbs from 31.4 to 96.5 percent. The reason is that major accidents are rare, and therefore there's not much "load" for administrative costs in a $250-deductible policy. On the $50-deductible policy, there's a tremendous amount of administrative expense that must be paid, eventually, by the policyholder.

annuity

The annuity is a guaranteed income per year for any number of years. But the income includes invasion of capital; i.e., at the end of the annuity period, there is no return of the initial investment. It has been spent. The insurance company can calculate the rate of payment based on the life expectancy of the annuitant. If you're sixty-five and the mortality tables say you have ten years to go, then the insurance company can count on paying you back your capital in ten equal installments, plus whatever interest and dividend income the company can earn on the capital in the meantime. Thus the rate of return on the typical annuity seems extremely high; however it is not all investment income, but a return of capital plus some investment income. The annuity is useful if you think you're going to live longer than the average. If you live too much longer than the average, however, you will find yourself trapped into a fixed income, which will continue to lose its buying power as inflation goes on. Remember that you can always do better than the insurance company as long as you can earn a better rate of return on your capital investment. You don't need to pay someone else to take your money and then hand it back to you. You can invest your capital directly, spend the investment income and part of the capital, too, and still do better than the annuity, as long as the remaining capital is invested at a higher rate of return than the insurance company gets. The return must be substantially higher, and it will surely have to come through capital appreciation. Remember, also, the hidden risk in annuities: if you die sooner than the average, your entire capital invested in the annuity is gone. I don't think annuities are the answer.

Blue Cross and such

The same principle that applies to collision insurance applies to medical insurance policies. Insurance is a very expensive way to save for routine, recurring, petty expenses. It *is* a very efficient way to handle the slight chance of suffering a major disaster. Do not buy Blue Cross policies. The only medical insurance to buy is medical-disaster insurance. This is *major medical* insurance and it's amazingly cheap, especially if you use the principle of self-insurance and insist on a high deductible, something on the order of $500. A typical relationship between deductible and premium would be this: premium of $200 for a policy with a $250 deductible; premium of $80 for a policy with $1,000 deductible. The major-medical policy with a high deductible is by all means the most efficient medical coverage.

over sixty-five

For ten years or so, Guardian Insurance has offered a policy for those over sixty-five who qualify for federal medical care. For $144 a year, they can get full coverage of medical costs incurred *after* they have exhausted the services of Medicare. If you're over sixty-five, this might be worth some research, depending on your individual circumstances.

term

Life insurance is intended to cover the risk of premature death. Obviously that risk gets smaller as your wealth grows bigger. Year by year the statistical odds increase that you'll die in the coming year. To buy a life-insurance policy that runs only one year, you pay a small premium in your younger days and a larger and larger yearly premium as times goes on. This permits you to match the size of the policy to the risk you wish to cover. There are dozens of different payment schedules, but the only genuine form of life insurance is term insurance, bought year by year (or perhaps in two-year policies) in amounts that meet your needs from time to time.

whole life

If you don't buy term insurance, then you wind up with some confusing combination of term insurance and savings plan. In a typical whole-life policy, you pay a fixed premium each year until you're sixty-five. At that time the insurance is "paid up," is yours if you die, and sometimes yours at a discount, if you want to take the cash (at that point it can be converted into various forms of annuity as well). But the flat premium is nothing but a variable-ratio term-plus-savings payment. In the early years you are giving the company a major portion of that premium simply to build up your savings account with the insurance company. Only a small portion covers the true risk and cost of your premature death. Once again the insurance company adds your excess payments to its investment portfolio, which is invested in government bonds and other securities that won't protect you against the damages of inflation. You would be far better to spend the same amount of money, but perform the investment management yourself; buy the term policy, but invest the difference in a portfolio that will give you more help in the battle against inflation. If your business and your portfolio are prosperous, you may find that you need less and less life insurance as the years go on, and that a level premium for term insurance will buy you just what you need—decreasing life coverage as your family finances gain headway over the years.

insurance brokers

Anyone can buy an insurance policy or set up an insurance program for your family. But don't kid yourself that the job is finished when that much is done. The job hasn't even started. All you have is a box full of pieces of paper that show that in certain circumstances a certain company promises to pay you something. How do you know the company will pay off without a fight? *Insurance doesn't start until the company pays off.* Thus the most critical element of your insurance program is your chance of collecting on your policies. For this reason you want to deal with a broker who can go to bat for you. A small broker who sells a few policies a year is not very important to insurance companies that count their policy values in billions. You need a larger broker whose business is important to the companies that issue the policies. I believe the two biggest brokers are Marsh & McLennan and Johnson Higgins. They have offices all over the world, and when they stand behind you, you can collect on your policies in a matter of days. It's no time to start haggling with some rat-eyed insurance investigator or "claim adjuster" when you're flat on your back in a hospital, or when your home is demolished. Deal with an old established house, a broker who can do you some good. That means dealing with one of the giants. When you need help, you can use *their* clout.

interest

There are several kinds of interest rates—effective, nominal, originary, and true (or "real").

effective

Effective interest is the quantity of interest paid on the average amount of loan outstanding during a given period. This is particularly important in figuring the interest rate on installment loans. If you borrow $100 and pay it back over a year in equal monthly installments, and if the interest charge added on is $9.00 the nominal rate of interest may be 9 percent, but the effective rate is twice that. On average, you will be *using* only $50.00 for the full year. That $9.00 interest charge is a full 18 percent of the $50.00 you get to use for the year. If the $9.00 is *discounted* up front (in a so-called discount loan, surely one of the least candid packaging labels ever invented), then you start with only $91.00 to use, your average loan for the period is $45.50, and the effective interest rate is 19.8 percent! Keep your eye on the cash. Find out how many dollars you'll have the use of, on average; find out how many dollars of interest charges you'll be paying; the ratio between those figures is the effective interest rate.

nominal

Nominal interest is the rate expressed in a number—5, 6, 7 percent. Because inflation may wipe out a portion of the capital invested, the amount of nominal interest does not measure the true position of the lender.

originary

We exist in time, and so do our wants. When we want something, it is implicit that we want it now, not a year from now. If we are given a choice between a satisfaction coming a year from now and the same satisfaction immediately, we always prefer the immediate satisfaction. In market terms, we will gladly pay a higher price for immediate satisfactions. There is always this difference in price between the present and the future good. The discount on the future good is called originary interest. From one society to another the originary interest rate will differ, in accord with each society's willingness to forego present satisfactions in order to increase future satisfactions (something done when current income is saved, converted into tools, and used to increase the productive efficiency of the society). In any given society the level of originary interest is the same for all goods.

true, or real
Nominal interest corrected for the effect of inflation on the buying power of the capital lent out is true or real interest. During a rapid inflation there may even be negative real interest rates, because the nominal interest does not compensate for the loss of buying power represented by the capital itself.

interim reports
Financial statements issued by companies at intervals of less than one year.

internal financing
Use of current inflows of funds for capital expenditures, funds from non-cash charges such as depreciation allowances, and from profits retained after taxes. Successful long-term growth companies traditionally rely heavily on internal financing.

International Monetary Fund
A multinational bureaucracy that attempts to control the monetary affairs of the world markets. The member nations, about 120 of them, contribute "deposits" to the IMF and have the right to borrow to cover deficits. But the main currency is the dollar, which has been in deficit for twenty years, and the IMF doesn't know what to do about it. The members meet several times a year in interesting cities

throughout the world, but the great international inflation continues.

inventory accounting

How to give a dollar figure to your business inventory? Evaluate the whole thing at the unit cost of the most recent addition to the inventory? That's LIFO (last in, first out). Evaluate the thing at the actual historical cost of each item? That's FIFO (first in, first out). And how about the value you place on goods in production, which may nevertheless never be sold because they're obsolete or because they don't work? When you study the corporate **balance sheet,** be aware of the various pitfalls in inventory accounting.

investment

Investment is 1) the act of using current income to buy tools to increase future income, or 2) the tools so bought. *Direct* investment is the purchase of productive tools. *Portfolio* investment is the purchase of securities that represent some form of ownership or claim in the productive tools. See also **gambling.**

investment banker

An investment banker or banking house is a firm that helps corporations raise new capital in the money markets. If a corporation needs a million dollars, it will negotiate the sale of a million dollars' worth of stock to an investment banking house (which may set up a group of other houses to share the risks of the venture). The corporation now has its money, the investment bankers are out a cool million, and it's now their job to turn around and sell those shares of stock to the investing public. The mark-up is hardly the 60 or 70 percent you find in retailing. Investment bankers work on margins more like 10 percent, depending on the risks inherent in the deal. If your broker works for a firm that also has a major investment banking business, make sure there's no conflict of interest. The best way to make sure is to ask your broker never to call you up with recommendations.

Investment bankers are also called *underwriters*.

investment club

Six or eight friends chip in a few dollars to start with and a few dollars at regular intervals, building up a kitty that they invest in a portfolio. Each member may have a special area of investments he is asked to investigate and report on. Stocks are selected on the basis of the research performed by the members and by a simple majority vote of the membership. The clubs are good for social fun, and they get a lot of people interested and active in educating themselves about financial matters. But they do not guarantee good results, because six or eight amateurs are hardly better than one, and we all know about decisions made by committees. Nevertheless, if the members are unable to raise enough money individually to get into the market, this is a way for them to get started. They're starting on the wrong foot, they're headed for a banana peel, but at least they're off dead center.

investment counselor

The investment counselor will manage your portfolio for you, on either a discretionary or non-discretionary basis. His charge should be about 1 percent of the average market value per year on the first $100,000 or $200,000 of market value, and lower on amounts larger than that. Most investment counselors have a minimum fee of about $2,000 a year, which inhibits the investor who has less than $200,000 or so in the market. There are some investment advisers who do not have a minimum fee and who manage to perform good service for accounts as small as $5,000. I am one of those. See also **advice.**

investment objectives

Each person has a different objective for his portfolio. Usually the investment objective is a compromise between the desire for immediate cash income and the desire to maintain purchasing power over a number of years. To minimize taxation, provide amusement and activity for a retired businessman, set up a fund for a child, finance an education starting five years from now—these can be investment objectives, too. The important thing is to know as precisely as possible what it is you're trying to do with your money. Once you have defined your goals, you can take rational steps toward reaching them. If you're fifty-fifty on income versus growth, why not invest 50 percent of the portfolio in high-yielding securities and 50 percent in long-term growth opportunities? Or, if you can specify exactly how much cash income you need from your portfolio, why not get that cash income from some high-yielding securities and put all the rest into long-term growth to fight inflation? If you have several different objectives, divide the funds into portions devoted to each objective exclusively. Then you'll avoid the trap of trying to pick securities that are all things to all men. Keep things simple and direct so you'll know what's going on and have some reasonable way to measure whether you're getting what you want out of your investment program. And if your objectives change, change your portfolio.

J

joint ownership
Not recommended as a standard form of ownership. If there are overriding reasons for holding some property jointly, be sure to keep extremely accurate records showing who paid how much for what. Otherwise, the tax boys can hit you with taxes on supposed "gifts" of a half-interest in the property.

K

kaffir
Any South African gold-mining company or its stock. One of the best investment vehicles for the 1970s and early 1980s—indeed, for the duration of the inflation spree.

keep your eye on the cash
Otherwise known as Rickenbacker's Rule. This little law helps you analyze financial statements and attempted swindles. If you know who pays what to whom and when, you know the guts of any financial transaction.

Keogh Plan
A retirement plan that permits a self-employed person to contribute $7,500 a year to his own retirement fund, to write off the contribution as a current deduction from taxable income, to invest, reinvest, and earn investment income within the fund, tax-free, until retirement—and then pay taxes on the funds withdrawn at presumably lower tax rates. For evaluation of such plans, see **retirement.**

Keynesianism
Economic system attributed to John Maynard Keynes, although he repudiated it late in life. It asserts that the economy is mature (as of 1932), that government can provide full employment by manipulating the interest rate, can manipulate the interest rate by controlling the money supply, and so on. The followers of Keynes have been in power for forty years and have not notably succeeded in their goals, providing the best possible confirmation of Keynes's own suspicions late in life that he had goofed.

L

labor unions
From the standpoint of the investor, unionism is a problem. Labor is a cost to the owner of the business. He would prefer to calculate that cost on the basis of market forces rather than on the basis of monopolistic practices. After a certain point has been reached in labor costs, further wage rises cannot be passed through to a higher selling price. Foreign competition enters the picture, then tariff barriers, favoritism, and government intervention on a grand scale. Better to use the forces of the free market as much as possible.

lawyers
Mark Twain used to define a gold mine as a hole in the ground with a lawyer sitting on top of it. My father used to pronounce "barrister" suspiciously like "bastars." A friend of mine—a bastar himself—says you'll find lawyers hovering about like buzzards wherever there's money. And since we're talking about money and making more of it, we're running a course that will throw us into the lawyers' arms whether we like it or not. Be prepared. Keep your arrangements simple and standard. Avoid tricky deals, fine print, trusts, foreign corporations, elaborate tax-avoidance schemes that cost a thousand dollars in bastar fees to save nine hundred in taxes. Never use a lawyer with a phony English accent. Get a young one who needs your business and isn't trying to build a new tennis court with your fees. Bear in mind he'll start the meter running as soon as you call him on the phone. One lawyer I used to know, who had

several children in school and college at the time, used to urge his partners to "keep the client on the phone as long as you can." An amiable wit, he would tell jokes, inquire about the family, comment on the news of the day, discuss politics (for he dabbled in it), invent complexities requiring further research. An amiable wit indeed. Get a local lawyer so that if he has to come to your place he won't charge a hundred dollars an hour for travel time. Keep things simple. Remember—complexity costs you *twice;* once when you pay the bastar fee to set it up, again when things go wrong because no one understood the deal in the first place.

let your profits run
In my observation this is where the big money has been made. You buy a stock because you think the company is going to do well over the long pull. It does do well. The stock goes up. You double your money. You treble your money. Should you sell out? The answer is a firm *no.* As long as the outlook remains fine, you should hold on and let those profits keep right on growing! That's the sign of the professional investor. The amateur does the opposite. As soon as he gets a nice profit, he sells the whole position, mainly to tell his friends about the great profit he made in the stock market. Naturally he never mentions that he would have made even greater profits if he had let his profits run. And naturally he doesn't mention what he did with the funds by way of reinvestment. Not so well, perhaps, or we would have heard of that too. The amateur sells his winners in order to look good and hangs onto the losers in the egocentric hope that they'll **turn around** and make him look good. After a few months or years of this, the amateur's portfolio is a collection of losers grimly retained by stupid pride. Look at the history of the amateur portfolio and you'll find a large number of trades that produced modest profits and a current list of holdings showing huge losses that wipe out the profits and then

some. The professional shows a larger number of trades closed out with negligible losses and a small number of positions currently held with substantial gains that are still going strong. Be a pro!

leverage

Leverage comes into play when a small change in one factor produces a large change in another. It can, of course, work for you or against you. There are two main types of leverage in financial analysis: capital leverage and operating leverage.

capital

Capital leverage occurs when the capital structure of a company is heavily in debt, and when most of the profits of the company are burned up paying interest on the debt. A small increase in profits can result in a large increase in the earnings or the common stock. There is no operating leverage: the profit ratio remains constant. Here's how it might look:

	Before	*After*
Annual Sales	$150,000	$200,000
Profit Margin	20%	20%
Gross Profit	$ 30,000	$ 40,000
Interest Expense	$ 20,000	$ 20,000
Earnings Available	$ 10,000	$ 20,000
(to stockholders/owners)		

In this case a 33 percent rise in gross profit, before interest expense, leads to a 100 percent rise in earnings on the common stock.

operating

Operating leverage exists when a company can increase its total revenues a large amount by only a small increase in expenses. Transportation companies are a classic example of operating leverage. An airline may be earning 5 percent on its capital while running its planes only half full. It won't cost any more to carry 20 percent more passengers. If those passengers can be found, and if the company started with a breakeven load factor of 45 percent, the profits would *double* while the number of passengers increased by only 10 percent! That's operating leverage. You'll find it in any business that has a high level of fixed costs, a low margin of profit, and the ability to handle increased business without a corresponding increase in expenses.

liabilities
Amounts that are owed to others.

limit order
An order to your broker authorizing him to buy or sell at a certain price (or at a more favorable price), within a specified period of time.

listed company
One whose stock is admitted for trading purposes on an organized securities exchange such as the New York Stock Exchange or the American Stock Exchange.

liquidity
A fancy name for cash. See **cash,** and remember that the first law is the keep your eye on it. Besides the simple definition as cash, and the discussion of cash reserves for the individual, there are a couple of ideas about liquidity that you should be aware of. These are corporate liquidity and portfolio liquidity.

corporate

Corporate liquidity is a special example of the importance of keeping your eye on the cash. The collapse of Penn Central Railroad was an excellent example of mass hypnosis by large figures. Penn Central kept borrowing and borrowing to pay its bills; lenders kept lending and lending because 1) they could earn a high interest rate, and 2) the loans were "secured" by the general faith and credit in a corporation whose balance sheet showed $2 *billion* worth of real estate—all that acreage in downtown Manhattan. But when Penn Central collapsed, it suddenly became evident that it's one thing to own land and buildings on Park Avenue and something else again to sell them and get the cash *now*. The idea of liquidity includes the idea of easy disposability. All those rocks on the back side of the moon may be worth millions, but they can't (or shouldn't) be used to secure or back up a loan. A corporation that shows a lot of assets but only a small amount of cash may *not* be as powerful as it seems. In fact, it *may* be on the brink of bankruptcy. An asset is worth only what you can sell it for. And, with a nod to the discussion of **originary interest,** the idea of sale implies sale *now*, not ten years from now after a prolonged battle in the law courts. You want to see a corporation whose assets are easily and swiftly saleable in an active and affluent market.

portfolio

Portfolio liquidity has to do with saleability of the assets in the portfolio. If you have a choice between two securities that are identical in every respect except for liquidity, choose the more liquid one. **Municipal bonds** are not easy to buy or sell before maturity. Some corporate bond issues do not trade in active or liquid markets; and it's not well known that the New York Stock Exchange makes little attempt to maintain an orderly market in its listed bonds.

Stocks traded **over the counter** are subject to dismaying softness in quotations when the general price structure seems to be sliding. If you've given sufficient attention to your own **cash reserves** of various kinds, the question of portfolio liquidity should not be crucially important. Allow plenty of time to sell the less liquid securities. Plan ahead, and never let yourself be put in the position of being forced to sell something quickly that isn't all that easy to sell. And when you evaluate your holdings from time to time, be sure to allow a discount on the less marketable items.

loan

Amount received from others under a promise to pay it back. See **car** and **home** for discussion of rental vs. ownership (rental is property received from others under promise to make payments in return). Temporary loans for emergency purposes based on savings-account passbooks are marginally reasonable. In installment and consumer loans, be sure to compute the real rate of interest (see **interest**). Prepayment of loans during a period of fast inflation is unwise unless you think you're unable to use the money at a better rate of return. If the real rate is 18 percent, as it most probably is, you're wise to pay the loan off as quickly as possible; few investment managers can guarantee 18 percent.

loan shark

Anyone who makes loans at illegally high rates and uses violence to collect payments. Note that the rates to marginal borrowers would probably be *lower* if the usury laws were scrubbed from the books—a perfect example of government intervention intended to protect, but which actually victimizes instead.

locked in

An investor says he's locked in when he owns stock that have gone up astronomically in market value; he figures he'd have to pay such huge capital-gains taxes if he sold that he'd have too little to reinvest to make the sale worthwhile. This is the counsel of despair. Even assuming the stock is worth ten times what he paid for it, the taxes on the sale would not make it impossible to reinvest and get the same income in almost every case. Furthermore, by using more sophisticated techniques in commodities trading, it is possible to defer the payment of taxes for years—until, in fact, the *new* investment has earned the money to pay for the taxes from the sale of the *old*. So: don't let the inevitability of taxes become a factor in poor investment decisions. The aim of the investor is to make profits, to pay the taxes on them, and to keep making more profits. I suspect that people who say they're locked in enjoy boasting about their big **paper gains.** As long as there's some other investment that promises to do better than the one you're in, there's no reason to be locked in. Keep moving.

long

In possession of. You're long a stock when you own it. See also **short.**

long-term holding

Under the tax law, any holding you've had for more than six months. It's taxed, if you show a profit, at lower tax rates than are applied to **short-term holdings** or ordinary income. Long-term holding is the preferred system for serious investors and is the broad avenue to success in the stock market over a period of years.

loss

Difference between your cash outlay, and a lower amount
of cash receipts from a complete transaction. *Capital loss*
occurs in capital transactions. *Tax loss* is a loss incurred and
reportable and deductible for tax purposes but perhaps not
incurred in real life (see **wash transactions**). *Stop-loss* is an
order to your broker, placed at a fixed price (a **limit order**),
to be executed if the security reaches that price, the whole
transaction taking place in order to limit the loss possible in
a given position.

low-priced stocks

Some stocks sell for hundreds of dollars per share. Others
sell for only a few pennies. Generally, stocks that sell for
less than twenty dollars a share are considered low-priced
stocks. There is a presumption against a low-priced stock,
because it may have taken a disreputable route to its low
estate. It might have been a **blue chip** in the good old days
that is struggling to stay alive now. Or it might have been
part of a cheap promotion: many low-quality companies
issue stock at a few dollars per share, simply because you
can always find an investor who thinks it a "cheap" price to
pay for a stock. For major analytical purposes, the price
of the stock doesn't matter. What does matter is the ratio between the price and the **earnings per share,** the
ratio between the price and the cash dividends, and the ratio between the price and the **book value.**

On a less fundamental level, there are some qualities that
are inherent in low-priced shares and not in higher-priced
ones: 1) As a percentage of money invested, the commission
cost is a bit higher when you buy low-priced stocks. 2) As a
group, the low-priced stocks are the last to get caught up in
a major upswing of market prices. After a great upsurge in
the prices of **blue chips,** you can speculate in the low-priced
stocks if you're particularly aggressive. But be careful: they
can drop like rocks.

M

management
What to look for in corporate management? 1) Balance between men who've worked all their lives for the company and men who bring outside experience to the company; 2) balance between younger and older men in top management (you don't want them all to drop dead at once); 3) well-conceived program to provide for replacement and succession in the top jobs; 4) candor in dealing with the press and stockholders. What to avoid? 1) Management by "family"—in-laws, cousins, nephews; 2) "stock-conscious" management—officers who are more interested in boosting the price of the stock than in producing the fundamentally sound business operation that is the only long-term guarantee of a healthy stock price; 3) a high degree of turnover in top management posts; 4) "one-horse" shops, where the top man boasts of handling everything himself, working twenty hours a day, never taking a vacation, and so on—a clinical description of poor management; 5) management that issues excessively complex financial reports; 6) evidence of "personal problems" among top men; 7) signs of excessive spending on status symbols; 8) excessive reliance on political influence to secure the company's prosperity. See also **board of directors.**

margin
Your equity in a brokerage account where the securities are used as collateral. A *cash account* at the brokerage house is one in which the securities are fully paid for.

margin call
If the market price of your securities should drop, they'll
have less value as collateral, and the amount of loan must
be increased. If your borrowings are already at the maximum allowed by government, you'll have to put up more
cash—more **margin.** Hence the margin call: death knell of
the underfinanced speculator.

market
Any two-way trading activity where buying and selling are
carried on.

at the market
During the business day, a certain stock may be bought and
sold in hundreds of different transactions by hundreds of
different people, with millions of shares changing hands.
The price moves up and down from minute to minute. You
can get quotes on the most recent transactions, but unless
you're right there on the floor of the stock exchange there's
always a lag of a few minutes. So, if you want to buy or sell
a stock, what should you do about this unstable price that's
moving up and down (even while you're trying to close the
deal)? The best answer is: do nothing, ignore the minor
moves. Many investors make a big mistake trying to pick a
price and ordering the broker to close the deal *when and if*
the stock hits that price (see **limit order**). Unless the investor
is just plain lucky, his order is never executed. I have seen
people refuse to buy a stock at 40 when the outlook is for it
to go to 100 in a couple of years—because they think they
can pick it up later at 35! They cheat themselves out of big
long-term profits in order to squeeze a nickel or dime out of
the opening transaction. The best advice, year in and year
out, is to order your broker to do the deal *at the market.*
This means your stock will be traded at whatever price is
necessary to bid or ask, in order to move the merchandise.

Why agonize? Selling a stock is like selling a used car: you get what you can for it, take the money, and look for fresh ideas. When you buy a stock, remember that if it's good at 35 it's also probably good at 40. A car won't drive off while you're haggling over the price, but a stock sometimes does. The great majority of your transactions should be *at the market.*

market letter
   See **advice: letters.**

market order
An order to your broker to execute the sale or purchase at the first available price. The order is "at the market," and it's the best way to go.

mathematical fallacy
The language of mathematics seems to be precise, but it contains hidden traps, especially when you try to apply mathematical reasoning to the real world. Consider $X = 2Y$. If you increase X, you will cause an increase in Y. If you increase Y, you'll cause an increase in X. Very good in algebra, but does it work in the real world? Suppose X is the amount of education going on in the country and Y is the amount of money being spent on education. Does X cause Y? Does Y cause X, in all circumstances? Equations are reversible: they work in forward and reverse gear just as well. The real world is causal and directional; a description of a coincidence does not prove the existence of a causal chain. A company spends 10 percent of its revenues on research. If it doubles its research budget, will it double its sales and profits? When you see arithmetic being applied to human situations (even if it's not in the language of arithmetic), watch out for the implication of a causal relationship that doesn't exist.

maturity
See **bond: maturity.**

maturity spectrum
If you own a variety of bonds, normally you'll try to have
them mature at different times, rather than having your
entire bond portfolio mature at once. The range of different
maturity dates, and the face amounts due thereon, make up
the maturity spectrum of your bonds. It's a schedule of the
funds as payable in the future.

merger
Two corporations join (merge) to form one corporation.
Usually the merger or surviving corporation begins to have
the features of a **conglomerate.** Better to sell the stock of a
corporation that's about to be merged, lest your position be
submerged.

monetarists
This is an unfortunate word, coined to describe nothing
more unusual than the truth about money. A monetarist is
anyone who understands that if you increase the supply of
money, you reduce the exchange value of it in terms of
other goods. In the autumn of 1896, in the little town of
Dawson, in Canada's Northwest Territories, the discovery
of gold nearby led to a great increase in the money supply
(which was gold) and a proportional drop in the exchange
value of that money. *Salt fetched its weight in gold.* The
relationship always holds. Increase the supply of money,
and you reduce its buying power in the marketplace.
Compare **money illusion.**

money

In one respect, money is like dress. See what people are wearing and you'll know what "dress" is being used in that place and time. Go to the market and see what people are using to make exchanges. If they're engaging in direct swapping of one good for another, they're using the *barter system*, and they have no money. If they're using something as an intermediate step between the sale of one good and the purchase of another, the thing in the middle is money.

Money takes many forms. Rocks have been used as money, as have sea shells, tobacco, cattle, salt, and dozens of other articles and goods. There are three main types of money: fiat, specie, and quasi-money. *Fiat money* is created out of nothing—printed paper—and is forced into circulation by government decree; it has no exchange value as a good in itself, and it can be undermined when the government issues too much of it. *Specie money* is money made from gold or silver or some other precious metal. It can be minted by commercial businesses or by governments. It will circulate on the basis of its metallic content as well as on the basis of any government decree concerning its exchange value. It can be inflated, as in Dawson (see **monetarists**), by sudden bonanzas, but such lucky strikes are infrequent, minor, and localized. *Quasi-money* is anything that changes hands "as if" it were money, though no one considers it "real" money; contracts are not written in terms of it, and important transactions are not conducted with it. Tokens, minor coins, unbacked bank deposits, and short-term debts and credits are quasi-moneys. A full tabulation of this kind of money would include money substitutes, commodity money, credit money, fiat money, token money, money certificates, commodity credits, and circulation credits. Human experience—our observation of what people do when they're given their own choice in the matter—shows that the preferable form of money is something useful in itself and rare enough to compress a lot of exchange value into a small object. The form of money that has brought the most misery to people throughout history is fiat money—such as the U.S. dollar.

money illusion
Irving Fisher, in a book entitled *The Money Illusion,* observed that during an inflation the financial community thinks prices are rising while the currency is remaining stable. Hence the hatred of the people is easily directed toward those who are charging "high" prices rather than toward the real culprits, those who are increasing the money supply.

money stocks
Some common stocks act like bonds because their dividends are so constant, so unlikely to rise, and so much like bond interest in predictability and safety. Hence, like bonds, these stocks tend to sell in accord with changes in the long-term interest-rate level. Examples are public utilities, telephone companies, and bank stocks.

money supply (Sprinkel)
Beryl Sprinkel has argued convincingly that there's a relation between the changes in the money supply and changes in the level of stock prices. He gives the theory that links the two events, then gives about forty years of statistics showing how the theory pans out in the real world. It seems to work.

moving average
An average made of consecutive elements in a series, and moving forward in time only a notch at a time, so that any given element occurs in more than one calculation of the average. This cancels out (or modifies) the effect of any one startling event, and produces a smoother curve on the

graph. But it also creates quite a time lag in identifying significant events. A company, instead of reporting each calendar quarter's results, might report every three months on the results for the most recent nine months, averaged on a three-month basis. Statistical juggling. Useful, but the raw numbers plus an explanation of any oddities might do just as well.

multiple of earnings
See also **earnings: per share.** The ratio of stock price to earnings per share is the multiple of earnings. In very broad average terms, the earnings multiple varies between 12 and 18, in normal times for normal companies. For many years IBM consistently sold at thirty times earnings. In the fall of 1974, many major companies were selling for four and five times earnings. The earnings multiple expresses the market's feelings about the future. It says, if it's low, "I know the company is doing well this year, but I don't think it can keep it up." The high multiple says, "I grant I'm paying a high price for this year's earnings, but look ahead and you'll see earnings rising at such a fast pace, and keeping it up for so many years, that today's purchase even at this price will be fully justified in a very short time." When you pay more than twenty times earnings, be prepared to hang onto the stock for the long pull.

municipal bond
See **bond: municipal.**

mutual funds
A mutual fund is a portfolio of investment securities held in the name of the fund, which is owned by people who have bought shares of the fund itself. There are two kinds of funds: closed-end and open-end.

closed-end

The closed-end fund is organized like a standard corporation. It has a definite number of its shares issued and outstanding. That number doesn't change except at long intervals, and the business is conducted with the fixed amount of capital raised in the past. Portfolios of mutual funds tend to grow in market value as the years pass. As the values increase, a certain portion of them represents a liability —the amount that will have to be paid in taxes on capital gains if the stocks are sold. Consequently the total market value of the portfolio is greater than the equity of the shareholders in the fund. The shares of the closed-end fund will tend to sell at a discount from the net asset value per share (the **book value**). Performance has been merely average.

open-end

The open-end fund is continuously engaged in selling new shares to the public, thereby raising new money, which it puts to work in its portfolio. It is also continuously ready to redeem its shares for net asset value each day. It runs its portfolio with an eye to making good investments, but has the additional handicap of being required to respond to the opinions of masses of people who may not have the best sense of timing in the world. Simply because the selling organization has been active and successful, or because the population thinks it's a wise time to invest, is no guarantee that the new assets flowing into the fund can be put to work profitably; it might be evidence that the time has come to sell rather than to buy common stocks. Simply because the sales force is on vacation, or the population is gloomy, is no reason why the portfolio should be sold. And yet the fund is required to put assets to work at times not of its own choosing, and to sell assets (in order to redeem shares) in unpredictable quantities at times when it should be buying instead.

Open-end funds have not performed well. One great exception has been International Investors, which has concentrated on gold-mining shares for many years. It is worth pointing out that the standard argument in favor of funds is that they provide you with diversification into hundreds of different companies. But statistical studies show that the job can be done adequately if you simply hold ten different stocks. (See **diversification**.)

Beware of the commission cost in buying an open-end fund. The selling company usually charges 8 percent of the money involved. That's a huge loss to swallow at the beginning. Redemption is at net asset value, without commission cost. Since you take an 8 percent beating on the first day, be prepared to hang on for a while!

N

natural-resource companies

During a prolonged and serious inflation, it's useful to emphasize natural resources in your portfolio, because they'll probably go up in price as the money goes down in purchasing power—and that will provide you with a measure of protection against inflation. There are various kinds of natural-resource companies.

coal

People are taking a more balanced view of ecology, and the Arabs are taking a more unbalanced view of the oil price, with the result that the outlook for coal is good. There are problems with management and with labor unions in this industry. I wouldn't go into coal too heavily; but if a stock can be found at a low enough price to offset the problems, it could work out well over a period of years.

land

Raw land, or land-development companies, have never suited my style. The claim is made that real estate is a great investment because its supply is limited. True, its supply in any given locality may be limited, but the number of people in that locality may actually decrease. People can move away. They can find uninhabited places and settle there. They don't have to buy the acreage you've been speculating in. Land-boomerism has been an American game since 1492. Over a long period of years, the average valuation of real estate has risen slowly, about in line with the decline of the money. That's an inferior performance.

Remember you have to pay taxes on real estate; it's a "negative-yield" investment. Real estate is expansible, too, because people can open up new territories. I'm sure the automobile expanded the usable real estate in this country by a factor of hundreds. Local speculations in land, based on local situations and local knowledge, can work wonders—as, for example, when your name is Astor and you're buying forest lands on Manhattan Island. You can also lose your shirt in real estate—as, for example, when your name is Flagler and your plans for Montauk or southern Florida are fifty years ahead of the times.

mining

Much better. Metal prices will tend to reflect the general loss of buying power of money, but they will also reflect the increasing demand for metals over the long run, as industrial society expands. Undoubtedly the best investments for the next several years will be in gold- and silver-mining companies, because the outlook for gold and silver prices is for them to rise strongly for some years—indeed, until the western nations learn how to manage a sound currency again. The bulk of the assets placed in natural-resource companies should be concentrated in the gold and silver positions.

oil

The oil business includes companies that are mere processors (refiners) and others that are natural-resource owners (crude producers). The great crude producers are in a position to manage and develop natural resources which are, in turn, indispensable in the modern economy. I have no doubt that the great international oil-producing companies will continue to prosper for many decades into the future. Their stocks should be above-average investments and should constitute the second-heaviest commitment in the natural-resource sector of your portfolio.

timber

Not all that good. It's not a disappearing asset. You can grow it, you know. And there are difficulties with labor unions and high-cost production methods. It's a nice going business, with a perennial outlook, but too cyclical and too average to merit investors' attention.

uranium

The coming thing. For the patient investor, this could be the growth industry of the century—the twenty-first century. Nicest way to play the uranium game would be to buy one of the several South African gold-mining companies that have a substantial uranium participation.

net assets

Total assets, minus debts payable. In a mutual fund, market value of assets minus any debts; this is the redemption price per share.

no-load

Absence of sales commission on purchase of mutual fund shares.

nominee

See **street name.**

nonrecurring items

Income statements should show the normal operating flow of receipts and expenditures. One-shot profits, occasional "acts of God," should be shown separately. Such nonrecurring items should not form part of the earnings basis on which the common stock will be evaluated. A company's treatment of nonrecurring items in its financial reports is a good test of its general reliability and honesty.

note

An IOU. Issued by the government, it's federal paper. Issued by a corporation, it's commercial paper. Issued by a bank, it's a certificate of deposit. Usually traded in batches of many thousands of dollars.

O

odd lot

Normally a stock is traded in transactions involving a hundred shares at a time. That's called a **round lot** and is the standard transaction size. It is possible, however, to buy less than a round lot (which is called an odd lot). One or two firms make a specialty of buying round lots and then breaking them into little pieces to retail to the odd-lot trader. There is a slight additional commission cost in trading odd lots, which goes to pay for the extra step involved. The extra commission is called the *odd-lot differential* and is about one-quarter of a point. One theory of market timing asserts that the general public deals in odd lots, and that the general public is always wrong. Thus when during rising prices, the odd-lot statistics show a great rise in the volume of trading, the theory predicts that prices will tumble, and vice versa. Like all seemingly mechanical theories of market behavior, this one depends upon intuitive interpretation of the data, and its results are of only average usefulness.

of record

When you buy a stock, the paperwork is actually completed on the fifth business day later—the *settlement date.* As of that date you're the official owner, the "holder of record." Dividends are payable from time to time to the holders of record on a certain future date. If you want to buy to catch the dividend, allow enough time to become holder of record before the "record date." (Or buy for cash—immediate settlement—and get the record date quicker.)

Old Man River companies
Remember the glorious song from *Showboat* about Old Man River, who "just keeps rolling along"? Well, there are companies that seem to do the same thing. Year in, year out, they do business as usual, avoiding major strikes, political assaults, international competition, technological obsolescence, raids, bankruptcy, and so on. These are companies with a humble product—salt, snuff, blue jeans, soy derivatives, midwest newspapers—and plenty of room to grow. No politician is going to mount a great publicity campaign to "clean up" the snuff business, and Ralph Nader won't attack the blue-jeans manufacturers, will he? These are companies with a low profile, low-priced products, and millions of customers, companies performing those everyday services that we'll need as long as we're human. If you can get a few of these stocks into your portfolio at reasonable purchase prices, you'll build a solid foundation in the industrial sector. Make sure they're going to grow at least as fast as the inflation rate, however.

operating profit
Profit from the normal operations of a business, usually figured before taxes, interest expenses, or other nonoperating costs. Operating profit as percentage of total operating revenues is the *operating profit margin,* a very good measure of the fundamental soundness of an operation.

option
Choice. A contract permitting the buyer a choice of future actions: to buy at a certain price before a certain date, or not to buy; to sell at a certain price before a certain date, or not to sell. See also **call** and **put.**

originary interest
See **interest.**

over-the-counter (OTC) market

The over-the-counter market is the general sum of brokerage activities in buying and selling unlisted stocks, which the brokers carry as their own inventory of stock in trade. They deal as principal, not as agent, and make their commission by selling at a slight mark-up.

overall return (portfolio)

Also called "overall yield" or "total investment yield," this is simply the sum of the cash income plus the capital gains (whether realized or not) in a portfolio. Suppose you start the year with a market value of $10,000 and receive $500 in dividends for the year. At the end of the year, the market value has risen to $11,000. Your total portfolio yield, or overall return, is 15 percent. That's a very reasonable goal to shoot at, by the way.

P

paper gain
The difference between what you paid for a stock and its higher current market price. There's a gain, but it's only "on paper" until you "realize" it by selling the stock and nailing down the profit. You can't eat paper gains. You can't eat percentages.

paper loss
See **paper gain,** and drive it in reverse. Sometimes you can convert a paper loss into a real one, in order to offset **capital gains,** thereby reducing your yearly tax bill. Your broker can show you how to nail down a paper loss without losing your position in the stock (if you desire to keep holding the stock). But beware of unnecessary shuffling around to escape taxes. Most such schemes do not avoid tax; they merely defer tax. Make sure that the transaction costs aren't out of proportion to the benefits you derive. You get the use of the money (the tax deferred) for a certain amount of time. If it costs 20 percent in transaction costs to get the use of the money for one year, you're better off borrowing at 18 percent and reducing your bookkeeping.

par
See **bond: par** and **stock: par.**

parlay
Using **paper gains** to finance loans which create profits used to finance further loans until the whole thing blows up in your face, which is exactly what most such schemes do.

payout (payout ratio)
The proportion of cash dividend as a percentage of total
earnings per share after taxes. The average payout ratio for
companies that have passed the early growth stage is about
65 percent.

penny stocks
  See **low-priced stocks.**

permanent investment
There is no such thing. See **growth** and **cycles.** Perhaps the
closest we can come to an investment that is permanent is
agricultural land. Until the next glacial age. But in everyday
terms, you should not consider any form of investment as
permanent. It is extremely hard to think of any company
that will be going strong, still growing, a hundred years
from now. Only a few of today's great companies will be
attractive as long-term investments fifty years from now.
You should constantly be alert for changing conditions that
will make you sell what you used to think was a long-term
holding. Times change. The unforeseen pops up. You should
be ready to respond with action. Don't freeze your reflexes
beforehand by permitting yourself to indulge the delusion
of permanence in your holdings.

personal factors
The kind of a person you are determines in broad outline
the kind of investment policy you'll have. The first requirement of your investment policy is that it permit you to get a
good night's sleep. Then, within the limits of what you can
live with, you must try to invest as wisely as possible in
these chaotic times. That's the normal situation of the timid
investor who forces himself to accept risk because he knows
that the old "safe" way of saving cash is now the least safe
way. But I have known the opposite extreme, the sporty

investor who thinks it's all a game, who loves to buy on a hunch and sell on a tip, but who realizes nevertheless that he should be doing something a little more sensible with his money. There's an interesting way to handle this kind of investor: give him a fraction of his portfolio, maybe a tenth of it, to "play around with" on his own, and put the remaining 90 percent of his investments into the kind of prudent, long-term, carefully built portfolio that he would never have the patience to build himself, even if he knew it was the thing for him. That little **play portfolio** that he runs for kicks will keep him happy—and, more importantly, it will keep his meddling hands away from the big stuff. There can be "sentimental" factors too. A stock you've held for a long time can come to be like a friend or a big brother. A stock that you've inherited may be hard for you to sell because "it was always good to Dad," or "Mama told me never to sell it," or "my uncle used to be friends with the guy who started that company," or "we buy their products," or "I used to work for the company." Sentiment has no place in your financial program. Stocks are not persons or puppy dogs. They do not reciprocate—and held blindly for foolish reasons, they can do you in.

pig
Old saying: Bears make money, bulls make money, but pigs never make money.

pink sheets
Daily publication of **bid** and **ask** prices for thousands of **over-the-counter** stocks.

play portfolio
Or toy portfolio, or play money. Small portion of one's fund to be managed for one's own amusement, in order to permit the bulk of the fund to be managed with an eye to

investment values rather than the thrill of it all. See also **personal factors.**

portfolio

Your portfolio is the collection of investments that you own. In tabulating your portfolio these days, you should include various other forms of wealth, such as **cash, coins,** or **bullion.** You don't have to be a millionaire to have a portfolio. Almost everyone has a portfolio whether he realizes it or not, and almost everyone's portfolio is inefficiently invested, or, at best, invested without sufficient regard to the dangers of long-term and accelerating inflation.

portfolio review (frequency)

It's not necessary to make a full-fledged statistical analysis of your holdings every day, because day-to-day fluctuations in prices are almost meaningless (see **random walk**). You should 1) read the financial news daily, 2) watch for any unusual events in the companies you own, 3) tabulate your market values once a month, 4) make a full review of costs, prices, yields, proportions (see **diversification**) once every three months. That'll keep you going just fine.

portfolio turnover
See **churning.**

preferred stock

This is stock that has first dibs on the earnings that are available for cash **dividends.** The preferred dividend is a fixed amount, like bond interest. Straight preferreds are seldom useful to individual investors. **Convertible** pre-ferreds can be quite attractive when the prices are right.

present value

The concept of present value rests on the idea that we always prefer a present satisfaction to a future satisfaction that is otherwise identical. The right to receive one hamburger a year from now will not cost as much as the right to receive a hamburger now. Put another way, tomorrow's goods sell at a discount today. And the further away tomorrow is, the greater the discount today. Thus the right to receive dividends forty years from now is worth very little compared with the right to receive dividends now. Because of this diminishing present value of future income, it is possible to buy and sell such things as common stocks, which represent the right to receive dividends forever. Stocks do not trade on the basis of the total sum of all future income figured at face amount. They trade on the basis of future income figured at a discount. Their price today is the present value of future income. See also **originary interest.**

price-earnings ratio
See **multiple of earnings.**

principal
1) Capital, not **income.** See **capital.** All principal is merely income saved. 2) Major party in a transaction, not the arranger, middleman, broker, or agent. In the stock market, when you buy through the services of an organized exchange, your broker acts only as your agent, arranging the deal with an unknown seller. When you buy **over the counter,** you may deal with a broker who is also the owner-dealer in the stock you buy, and who sells you the stock out of his own inventory position. He may choose to tell you that you pay no commission. But don't let that persuade you that he hasn't earned a piece of the action. If you sell him the stock you just bought, he'll only offer you about 95

percent of the purchase price. In effect, his "commission" is a mark-up on the merchandise. All perfectly normal. The difference between his bid and his offer is the **spread.**

prospectus
A full description of the facts and figures relating to an issue of new securities. The prospectus is required by the SEC. It creates a feeling that all is well ... which feeling has often proven to be misplaced. See also **registration.**

put
An option to sell a certain stock at a certain place before a certain date. See also **call** and **option.**

pyramid
See **parlay.** An idle dream. Don't try it.

Q

quality vs. price

It is not true that low-priced stocks are a better buy than high-priced stocks. The opposite is more likely to hold true, that high-priced stocks offer you more per dollar than the cheapos. Stocks are like diamonds. They sell on the basis of their substance. A one-carat stone sells for about half the price of a two-carat stone, but isn't necessarily a better bargain. Don't let the price per share influence your decision. Buy on the basis of the ratios: **earnings** per dollar of stock price, **dividends** per dollar of stock price, **book value** per dollar of stock price, **sales** per dollar of stock price. See also **low-priced stocks.**

quick ratio

The acid test of financial health: the ratio of cash assets (including near-cash like Treasury bills) to the total of current liabilities. A quick ratio of one-to-one is very good. Quick ratios of three or four might indicate a dying company that has no further use for the cash it is generating from operations.

quotes

You can ask your broker how a stock is doing and he'll give you what's called a quote. That's a report on the current market situation in that stock. The bid might be, say 35, and the ask 35½. That means you can sell stock at 35 and buy it at 35½. The broker will use jargon: "Thirty-five to a half, last a quarter." Translated: bid 35, offered at 35½, last sale was at 35¼. The quote does not guarantee a steady price for a huge transaction. It is valid for at least one round lot. After that, the quote may change in order to accommodate the new balance of supply and demand. You can also get the *size* of the market—how many shares are offered at 35½, how many shares at 35. For the average investor, such concern with the smallest details of the market condition is misplaced. I find it practical to put in a market order to buy or sell at whatever price we can get, because for the most part I deal in long-term investment positions, which are based on the prospect of substantial changes in market prices, and don't require haggling over the last quarter-point. Many a good investment has been missed because the investor refused to pay 35½, insisted on trying to buy at 35, and missed the ride to 70. If there's doubt, get a quote; but make it your standard to trade at the market. See also **bond quotes.**

R

rally
An upturn in prices that merely interrupts a longer and more substantial general drop in prices. Rallies during bear markets tend to be sharp, steep, and short-lived. They can catch you asleep. By the time you buy, the market has resumed its downward course. That's a "bear market rally," or a "bear trap."

random walk
Economists have fed forty years of market quotations into their computers and discovered that there's no pattern at all in the day-to-day changes in stock prices. Prices go up or down from day to day as if they were bouncing at random. It's this research, more than any other factor, that destroys the claims of the "chartists" or "technicians," who profess to see patterns in price changes, and who spend a lot of time announcing their predictions to the unwary. From day to day, price changes are totally unpredictable, but remember, they're also minor. The major movements in stock prices occur over a period of years and are closely related to the changes in the underlying operations and results of the companies involved. A company with good long-term growth prospects will have a stock that is likely to go up in price over a period of years. And that's about all we really know about stock prices! See also **security analysis.**

rare coins
See *coins.*

rate
Interest. Ratio between interest paid and capital invested, on an annual basis.

ratings
Bonds are "rated" according to the creditworthiness of the issuer, the funds available for repayment of **principal,** the flow available for payment of **interest** (debt service), the risk of the enterprise, the instability of the market, and so on. Moody's and Standard & Poor are the principal independent sources of bond ratings. The lower the rating, the greater the risk, and the higher the interest rate.

real estate
Portfolio investment in real estate is not recommended. Direct investment—in a few country acres, a farm, or a residential plot (which may have a house on it)—can be profitable. In my own opinion, real estate of all sorts is a below-average investment, if you consider the national real estate market as a whole. From coast to coast, great sections of major cities represent long-term bear markets in urban real estate values. In times of drought or plague, great areas of the country represent price disasters for agricultural land. If you have enough knowledge of a highly local condition (and perhaps a few friends in city hall), you can buy land that's right in the path of a major development and profit immensely. Most people, however, buy real estate with the twin objective of enjoying it as a family seat, and disposing of it later at a profit. The total investment yield must be figured on the basis of this conglomerate holding: one piece of land that provides recreation and *Lebensraum*, which are not quoted at the market, figured in your income, or taxable; plus providing a possible speculation on market prices. Only the individual can make such calculations. The costs should be figured also: taxes, mainte-

nance, alternative yields foregone. One great argument against using real estate as an investment is the difficulty of figuring out whether you really make a profit on it or not. See also **natural-resource companies.**

realized vs. unrealized (gain, loss)
See **paper gain** and **paper loss.** Unrealized gain is paper gain. Realized is the result of actual transactions for cash.

regional exchanges
The New York Stock Exchange and the American Stock Exchange handle a lot of business, but together they list only the three thousand largest companies. Twenty thousand other companies are traded in the OTC market and in regional exchanges like the Midwest, the Intermountain, the Spokane, the West Coast, the Baltimore, etc.

registered representative
  See **broker.**

registered securities
Securities that have passed through the SEC's registration requirements. See **registration.** This is only a requirement that certain facts be published. It is not a certification that the securities are of investment calibre.

registration
The Securities and Exchange Commission (SEC) was established in the 1930s with the ostensible purpose of protecting investors. Two of its principal functions are the registering of new investment securities and the registering of investment advisers.

investment advisers

In general anyone who proposes to sell his investment advice to the public must file a report with the SEC giving details of his proposed activities. He need have no special training. If the SEC doesn't interfere after the passage of a certain amount of time, he's in business. He can even advertise that he's "registered with the SEC"—an announcement that sounds like the Good Housekeeping Seal of Approval, but means nothing at all. The investor may even be gulled into thinking he's safe with an adviser who's registered with the SEC. To that extent, the legislation may do more harm than good.

new issues

The SEC requires a tremendous amount of information to be filed on proposed new issues of stocks or bonds. This was intended to reduce the number of shoddy or fraudulent issues sold to the public. If the SEC legislation and the registration procedures have been effective, then we should expect that the price experience of new issues in the forty years following the birth of the SEC would be, on average, better than the price experience of new issues before the SEC was founded to "protect the investor." Professor George Stigler actually measured the results of several hundred issues brought out before and after the SEC, and discovered that there is no measurable difference in the experience of the investor in new issues.

The existence of the registration requirement has given everyone a sense of confidence that is apparently unmerited and unwarranted. If there is any concrete result of the legislation, it is that new small companies find it harder and harder to start up in business. The registration with the SEC usually costs $250,000 in legal and printing costs alone. Remember: when you see that a new issue is "registered with the SEC," don't leap to the conclusion that Mama approves of your new love. It's just a legal formality, required, expensive, and, according to the good professor's findings, statistically meaningless.

resistance level
Although the graph of stock prices doesn't predict anything with cogency (see **random walk**), it can still be used in conjunction with other kinds of information. For example, time and again, I have seen the price of a stock drop year after year until it reaches a level that seems to be the absolute bottom, where the price is impervious to any bad news. Wars may come and go, lawsuits may be filed, the earnings may disappear, the company may start reporting deficits, the management can die of bubonic plague: the stock price refuses to drop further. This looks like a genuine resistance level and it is the signal for further investigation. If you find trends at work in the company that will eventually permit it to bail itself out of its difficulties, then you can buy with confidence that you have probably caught the bottom price, and it's all peaches and cream from then on. The same, in opposite colors, holds for top prices, when good news no longer succeeds in boosting the price of the stock. But please note that the price action is not the primary or exclusive signal. In conjunction with outside factors, it can help you make a decision or trigger your investigation.

retained earnings
Profits after taxes and payments of cash dividends. Such profits are held in the business and used for further development.

retirement

The most difficult financial problem for the ordinary person is planning for retirement. Pension benefits from the employer may be very important. Social Security will be of diminishing importance when it becomes clearer that the system is bankrupt. A private portfolio of investment securities, especially if they're able to produce steadily increasing cash income, should be of prime use. Keogh plans and similar ones that permit you to contribute a small sum each year (tax free) toward your retirement are valuable only if you start them very early (in your twenties) and invest successfully for thirty or forty years. The Keogh Plan permits a self-employed person to contribute $7,500 a year to his retirement fund, to take that $7,500 as a deduction from taxable income in the year contributed, and to earn and reinvest income within the retirement fund free of taxes. Taxes are paid when the person begins withdrawing from the retirement fund—i.e., during retirement, when presumably his tax bracket will be lower. Under a new Internal Revenue Service ruling, the Individual Retirement Account is available at many banks, but it's not available to the self-employed, to members of an established pension plan, or to members of a profit-sharing plan. If you qualify for an IRA account, you can contribute $1,500 a year, take that amount off your taxable income, and have the same tax treatment when you retire—i.e., pay taxes on the withdrawals during your retirement years and at presumably lower rates.

These plans look nice at first glance but they have their problems. Let's examine a typical offering. A bank is currently offering an IRA program at 7.75 percent interest, compounded, which produces a true interest rate of 8.17 percent. Now (see **Rule of Seventy-Two**) that rate of interest will double your money every nine years. If you start at age thirty and retire at sixty-five, you'll double your money four times—to sixteen times the average amount contributed. If you put aside $1,500 a year for thirty-five years, you will contribute a total of $52,500 and your average amount invested would be $26,250. Sixteen times $26,250 is $420,000—and that's almost exactly what the bank is offering you at age sixty-five. If you withdraw any funds before reaching retirement age (which can be as low as fifty-nine and a half under present law), you must pay taxes on the accrued earnings, *plus a penalty of 10 percent.* If you die before retirement, your beneficiary can receive the funds without penalty tax, though there would be the normal estate taxes. So you'll have a substantial penalty for trying to make the funds liquid before retirement. You'll have a guarantee of only 8.17 percent interest, although it's quite reasonable to shoot for almost twice as much total portfolio yield in a direct portfolio investment program. If inflation speeds up and interest rates keep rising, you'll be the loser. All such programs, which involve an "official" interest rate, are guaranteed to leave you unprotected against the dangers of further inflation. The statutory interest rate which they promise to pay is based on today's inflation rate. Inflation is almost certain to speed up; tomorrow's interest rates will be higher; yesterday's retirement programs, based on 5 percent rates, are already inadequate; today's are obsolete. And what about the bank that offers this interest rate for the next thirty-five years—is there any assurance that it's sound? Doesn't it have its own portfolio invested in long-term mortgages on residential and industrial properties that might or might not go broke? The bank may have cash assets of only a fraction of 1 percent of its liabilities. Suppose people wanted to get their cash all at once? Where would you be then? You'd own a deposit in a bankrupt company, and even if you could get your money out, the IRS would slap a 10 percent penalty on you for doing it! Looks as if the law was written for the benefit of the banks!

Insurance companies offer retirement plans that operate generally on the same principles, but there's one class of insurance policy that involves investing in common stocks. These policies are called *variable annuities* because the income will vary with the fortunes of the economy and of the companies the cash is invested in. But why hire the middleman? If the best answer to inflation is investment in long-term growth companies, why not save your money, invest it yourself, and get 100 percent of the benefits?

Retirement homes are not a special problem. Basically they either charge a flat fee, or they ask you to donate your capital in its entirety. If you have invested your capital wisely, it is far better to receive the income from your investments, pay the retirement home its monthly bill, and retain full control of your life—choice of investment, choice of retirement home (you're not locked in), and choice of beneficiary for your estate. Avoid all programs that involve a statutory interest rate. Keep as much control over your funds as possible. We are heading into highly chaotic times. Programs that involve a contractual relationship stretching thirty-five years into the future are hardly justified in conditions of zero forward visibility. There is, finally, no way to shift the burden of retirement. One way or another, your retirement income will represent the income you have refused to spend during your active years, plus the investment return it has earned in the meanwhile. Retirement is fundamentally an investment problem, and it's solved by doing the best investment job you can.

retreat
The voices of panic are heard in the land; there are men running about the country preaching the end of civilization; exhorting us to sell everything, scurry away to a cabin in a hidden valley in the mountains, plant a bean patch, and keep our ammunition dry so we can shoot the "revenooers" when they show their "haids." Well. All of that, mind you,

is urged in the name of maintaining one's standard of living.
It is a child's dream. Leave it to the children.

return on investment
  See **yield.**

revenue
Receipts from normal operations. See also **bond: revenue.**

risk
Risk is the possibility of loss. It thrives on uncertainty but
can exist alongside a clutch of certitudes too. You can, for
example, own a government bond that promises you a
certain interest rate to maturity. There is no risk about the
payments; they will be made on time. But there are two
risks inherent in the situation: 1) the risk of loss of buying
power, and 2) the risk of loss of *alternative* profits from
other investments that might do substantially better than
government bonds. It is impossible to invest without risk.
You must simply manage the risks so that they do not
overwhelm you, keep you awake at night, or force you into
erroneous, panic decisions. Almost everything is uncertain
and risky. Why should you expect investments to be any
different?

risk-reward ratio
This calculation was one of the inventions of the go-go
years on Wall Street. You assign a degree of risk, from zero
to one hundred, to a contemplated investment. You assign a
degree of reward, also from zero to one hundred, or from
32° to 212° Fahrenheit if you prefer, including your
estimate of cash yield, maximum appreciation potential,
and probability of achieving the maximum. Then you place
one number over the other, perform the problem in long
division, carry it out to two or three decimal places (to give

it an appearance of scientific exactitude) and—*voilà!*—the risk-reward ratio. Sheer balderdash.

round lot
Usually, one hundred shares. That's the normal size of a stock trade, as one dozen is the normal size of a transaction in eggs. Smaller trades are **odd lots.** There's a slight extra cost when you buy less than a round lot.

round trip
Buying in and selling out. In-and-out traders figure their transaction costs per round trip. They cut it pretty fine.

Rule of Seventy-Two
Extremely useful way to figure compound interest. How long will it take your money to double if you invest it at 6 percent, keep reinvesting the interest received, and earn 6 percent on all reinvestments? Simple. Use the Rule of Seventy-Two: divide seventy-two by the rate of interest and you get the number of years it takes to double your capital. Seventy-two divided by six is twelve. You'll double your money in twelve years. And remember: in twenty-four years you'll quadruple it, because you double it twice.

runaway inflation
See **inflation.**

S

safe deposit box
Most banks have individual boxes you can rent in their vaults for safekeeping of your valuables, contracts, securities, and so on. The normal family should be able to get along on a box that rents for about twenty-five dollars a year. You're the tenant of the box, and the bank can't refuse you entry during business hours. Few people understand this. They think that if the banks close, as they did in the 1930s, they won't be able to get to their safe deposit boxes. People had access to their safe deposit boxes during the "bank holiday." They probably will again—if the banks close.

safekeeping
Most brokerage firms will provide safekeeping services for your securities, even if they're registered in your name, without additional cost to you. This is a good way to hold the securities, because you avoid the trouble of running back and forth to the bank vault every time you buy or sell.

savings account
For investment considerations, see **cash.** Savings accounts pay different rates of interest in different states. They are "insured" to a certain extent, but only if there is no general panic; the assets of the insuring agency (a federal corporation) are insufficient to insure the whole amount of deposits. Withdrawals from savings accounts may be subject to legal delays, although in normal times the savings banks prefer not to advertise their legal right to require thirty-day or ninety-day notice for withdrawals.

savings & loan associations (S &Ls)

Mortgage warehouses. The S&Ls collect small amounts of money and promise to pay them back in a short time. They pool them into large amounts of money (mortgage loans) and loan them out to people who promise to pay them back in thirty years. Naturally, if the people who lend to the S&Ls want their money back, the S&Ls go broke. This is a classic example of that old and unsound banking practice, "borrowing short and lending long." I don't recommend anyone's making deposits in S&Ls. Too risky!

science and technology

I have rarely seen anyone make money by investing in stocks that have an interest in "new technology." Who can evaluate the *financial* benefits from a company's developing, say, an improved transistor? Why should you suppose that a company that can design a perpetual motion machine can also produce it and sell it at a profit? Why assume that only small companies with new products are going to benefit from the constantly expanding universe of man's techniques and knowledge? There are the brilliant exceptions, of course—on both sides of the fence. But it seems more prudent to invest in companies that have a proven record of developing new products and bringing them profitably to market; companies that regularly devote a large share of their revenues to further research and development work; companies whose sales are largely the result of products introduced in recent years. It is foolish to invest in a small new company that has one gizmo to its credit, when you can buy an established operation that has hundreds of gizmos, developed in its own labs over the years, for sale in established sales channels. If you insist on buying a new-gizmo producer, beware the One Great Problem: engineers and scientists who think they know how to run a company. For every genius like Dr. Land (who not only invented the Polaroid but built the company), there are thousands of inventive geniuses who have run their companies into the ground like absentminded professors. Word to the wise!

seasonal cycle
Seasonal ones come and go with the orbit of the earth around the sun. There's a retail boom at Christmas. Beer sales pick up when the warm weather comes. The price of gold drops when the International Monetary Fund meets in September to denounce the price of gold. See also **cycles** and **trend.**

secondary market
After a new issue has been sold to the public, a market will develop in which the new shares are traded from hand to hand after the original purchasers have sold them. That's the secondary market. Sometimes called "after-market."

secular trend
Any development that lasts more than a few years. See also **cycles** and **trends.**

Securities and Exchange Commission (SEC)
Federal watchdog. No statistical evidence in forty years that it has done any good. See also **registration.**

security
1) Certainty, of which there is none in financial matters.
2) Certificate of proportional interest (stock) or face-amount claim (bond, note). See also **certificate.**

security analysis

Security analysis is the work of selecting investment securities on the basis of *fundamental* or *technical* factors. The so-called technical factors turn out to be nothing more than a record of the market price of the stock over a period of time. Far from being technical, the system of graphing stock prices (always misnamed "charting") depends upon the most vague sort of intuitive judgments, and whatever detailed scientific evidence there is on the subject leads to the categorical conclusion that so-called "technical" or "chart" analysis is so much hogwash. See **random walk.** As for the other—and classic—school of security analysis, the so-called fundamentalist sticks to the same things that businessmen look at when they're buying and selling companies. This approach calls for detailed knowledge of products, prices, innovations, competition, financial resources, quality of management, prospects for growth, and so on. The fundamental approach has the virtue of aiming at the real world, but it's difficult to acquire knowledge not already acquired by someone else, and therefore already built into the price of the stock. Fundamental analysis is marvelously useful in establishing long-term investment positions. Like the technical, however, it is completely useless for predicting short-term swings.

selling losers

This is the sign of the professional. Don't hang onto a loser just because you hope it will go back to where you bought it so you can sell it without loss of face. Your vanity is no guarantee that the stock price will rise. Your capital is far better employed in an effort to maximize the investment return than in an effort to assuage your pride. See especially **let your profits run.**

settlement date
The fifth business day after the transaction date.

shares
  See **stock.**

shareholders
Shareholders are invited to the annual meetings of the companies. They can vote on the slate of candidates for directors. Nothing of note happens at the meetings, and the votes are Communist-style approvals of captive candidates. *But:* if you can amass enough shares to wield voting control of the corporation, you can take over. Occasionally a "corporate raid" will occur when outsiders buy enough stock to rock the boat. Then the fur flies! When that happens, bid adieu, serious investors. They don't want to get caught in the middle.

short
To be short is to be in debt. You can actually sell something you have borrowed, hoping to buy it back later at a lower price. You can sell stock short. Unfortunately, capital gains made from successful short sales are taxable at full normal income tax rates. Short sales are tricky to arrange because they must be made at a price *higher* than the next preceding different price—i.e., the short sale must be made "on the uptick." While you're short, you have to reach into your own pocket to pay cash dividends on the stock you have "sold." This is because you've actually created additional shares. The real owner of the shares you borrowed still collects dividends on his shares. The shares you sold short aren't paying dividends from any company, but the buyer has every right to receive them from someone—and the lucky guy is you. So short-selling is a tough business. I don't recommend it to beginners. See also **long** and **hedge.**

And not to get caught short, that's the long and the short of it.

short-term holding (trading)

The short term, for tax purposes, is anything less than six months. Short-term profits are taxed at ordinary income tax rates. Successful short-term trading is as much an art as a profession. The most successful practitioners seem to have some combination of expert knowledge of a small field and close acquaintance with people in the know. Find six or eight stocks you can deal with successfully, and stick with them.

silver

Silver has been the most widespread form of money throughout history. Like gold, it's a highly useful metal, in industry as well as the arts. Unlike gold, silver is used in a great variety of applications where it is unrecoverable. There's a spot of silver in every electrical contact and switch. There's a lot of silver in outer space, going on forever thanks to NASA and us taxpayers. It isn't practical to melt down ten television sets to get an ounce of silver. The industrial and commercial demand for silver runs a couple of hundred million ounces per year. The production of new silver from the mines is far below that. Indeed, the total demand for silver (including jewelry, hoarding, dentistry, and all that) exceeds the fresh production of silver by a couple of hundred million ounces a year. In the face of this continuing deficit, you might wonder why the producers don't respond to market trends and increase their production of silver. There's a good reason: they can't. About three-quarters of all silver is mined by people who are not in the silver business. It's mined as a by-product of people who are mining lead, zinc, copper. The price of lead and zinc and copper has more to do with the production rate of silver than the price of silver! So the above-ground supplies of silver have been gradually sold off. Old silver coins are being melted down. Speculative holdings are being sold. The Treasury has sold its once immense hoard of more than two billion ounces. The world is getting along— for the moment.

But the day is clearly visible when silver will be in demand and the supply will dry up. At that time the price will begin to rise. In the last ten years, the silver price has risen from $1.29 an ounce to $5.00 an ounce. Some enthusiasts foresee a price of $12.00 an ounce within a few years. Anything is possible when, because of perpetual inflation, the dollar sign itself is losing its meaning. And it is undeniable that there are supply-demand factors in silver, in addition to the inflation-haven features silver shares with gold. It is possible to make a case for silver being preferable to gold as a long-term shelter from inflation. You should be aware, however, that silver is an *industrial* metal, suffering from the ups and downs of industrial cycles, subject to reduced demand as the price rises, and exposed to competition from substitute metals when economics proposes so. Although the long-term outlook for silver might be better than for gold, the long-term investor in silver should be prepared for a far more exciting time of it than the long-term holder of gold. A prudent investor would make sure he had satisfactory positions in both metals, held for the long term, for the purpose of preserving the buying power invested in them.

bullion

You can buy silver bullion from a huge variety of sources, including many commercial banks. I'm not particularly hot on that idea, though; for the same reason I'm not eager to get involved with gold bullion. Storage charges, lack of divisibility, difficulty of assay, questionable liquidity in crisis: these are real drawbacks.

coins

Silver coins might serve you far better than bullion in protecting the liquidity and buying power of your funds. As with gold, I would avoid rare and precious coins and concentrate on the most widely recognizable and spendable form of silver coin. To my mind that means the splendid old silver dollar, preferably the circulated coins that can be bought for only a slight premium above their bullion value. Almost everyone recognizes a silver dollar and almost everyone realizes that the coin is worth far more than one dollar by now. The silver dollar contains about 77/100 of an ounce of pure silver; so you can figure its bullion value quite easily. Just look at the current market price of silver bullion. If it's $5.00 an ounce, then the silver dollar contains 77/100 of $5.00 worth of silver—or about $3.75 worth. In practice you should be able to buy silver dollars in quantity for about 10 or 15 percent above bullion content.

mining stocks

Silver-mining companies do exist, although most of them have substantial operations in other metals, and it's hard to get a silver stock that's truly concentrated in silver. The same kind of **operating leverage** exists in silver as in gold-mining stocks. With the long-term outlook quite favorable for the price of silver, it stands to reason that the mining shares should enjoy a good ride upward over the years. Beware the strong labor union structure, however, and occasional evidence of shady management. One of the most interesting securities in the business is the convertible debenture of Sunshine Mining. If you can get it below par, to yield 7 or 8 percent, you will receive a nice little income while waiting for lightning to strike the price of silver.

simplicity

Complexity is the happy hunting ground of the swindler. Beware of annual reports or registration statements that contain too much fine print, too many "notes to financial statements," or too many cross-references and interconnections that cancel each other out (or seem to). Beware of business enterprises (see **conglomerates**) that are too complex to be easily identified or described. Beware of financial structures that defy analysis (A owns 50 percent of B, B owns 55 percent each of C and D, C and D each own 26 percent of A; who owns whom?).

Beware of complexity in your own financial affairs. Keep ownership simple—don't fuss around with joint property, trusts, fancy insurance policies that promise compound benefits that can't be separated and individually analyzed, unnecessarily diversified portfolios, deposits in foreign banks, multiple accounts, and so on. Struggle toward cleanness, directness, simplicity. These are the great lasting virtues. One should add, however, that complexity may on occasion be admirable and fair.

special situation

A special situation exists whenever one company has a chance to stand out against its industry, or one industry has a chance to buck the national trend. Railroading may look like a thing of the past, and rail stocks may sell at discouragingly low prices, but you can find "special situations" from time to time that are worth your while, even in rail stocks. For example, how about the vast increase in the movement of coal, which will benefit the "Pocahontas" rails that shuttle between the Appalachian coalfields and the east coast ports? Even in a depression some industries can prosper mightily: gold mines, for example, or infant industries riding such a powerful growth curve that a slowdown doesn't even hit them. Don't look for too much in these cases. Even if you're right, a special situation may not go through the ceiling. If rails, on average, are selling for seven or eight times earnings, and you see an opportunity in the coal-hauling rails for something special, don't expect your stocks to go to thirty or forty times earnings. You are mainly riding the expected increase in earnings, which you shouldn't expect the market to evaluate at a multiple much higher than that accorded to the industry average. The higher earnings may even be priced at a slightly lower multiple, if the market thinks the high earnings are only temporary. Don't get into a special situation unless you have a good idea beforehand of what the signals might be to sell and take your profits.

specialist
A member of the stock exchange whose job it is to match up the buy and sell orders in a given stock, figure out a price that "clears" the market, and keep things going. At times he'll buy and sell for his own account in order to keep some degree of continuity in the prices of successive transactions.

speculation
See **gambling.** Not devil-words.

spin-off
When Company A owns all the shares of Company B, it will sometimes want to get rid of Company B. It can do this by simply distributing the B shares to the holders of the A shares, pro rata. That's called a spin-off. Normally, in a spin-off, you get something you didn't want in the first place. So sell the shares received.

sponsorship

Sponsorship is the *quality* of investment banking firms that underwrite a new issue or that make a market in an **over-the-counter** stock. If a small firm with no particular breeding underwrites a new issue, avert your gaze. If you're thinking of buying an over-the-counter stock and find that it's traded by only one or two small and undistinguished houses, watch out. Stick with the merchandise of the top-quality firms. There are about thirty of these firms, and any broker can give you their names. Or simply look at the names of the underwriters of the next large stock or bond issue from a blue-chip company. The gang's all there. Sponsorship is something more substantial than snob value. It stands behind the company whose stock is offered. If the company runs into unforeseen trouble, a small underwriting firm may not be able to help it. A group of large firms might supply extra managerial help to the company, arrange additional financing, create a climate of understanding and patience among the investment analysts, and with its prestige and heft generally strengthen the viability of the company. This means that the investor stands a better chance of avoiding disaster. It's like the difference between buying from a large department store with a standard refund policy and buying from a peddler you may never see again.

spot price

In **commodities,** the price of the commodity for immediate delivery.

spread

A difference between prices of substantially the same things. Happy hunting ground of the **arbitrageur.**

stabilization crisis
Final stage of hyperinflation. It no longer is possible to trade the useless currency for anything of value. People refuse to accept it. The economy must find a substitute currency that will have a stable exchange value. This is the stabilization crisis, the moment when the old inflation comes to a halt, a new currency is introduced—and, more often than not, the new inflation commences on little cat feet, 1 percent at a time.

stamps
Same investment judgment as for rare coins. See **rare coins.** Stamps have the additional problem of being easily lost or destroyed.

statistics
Beware statistics. They are the result of mathematical manipulations (see **mathematical fallacy**) that may or may not describe the real world. You can drown in a river that's only an inch deep "on average." You can suffer terrific downturns in a stock that gains 10 percent a year "on average." Beware of percentage figures that are the result of taking an average of other percentage figures. Example:

Sales Revenues

	1974	1975	Per cent Increase
Division A	$10,000,000	$10,500,000	5%
Division B	5,000,000	5,500,000	10%
Division C	100,000	1,000,000	900%
COMPANY	$15,100,000	$17,000,000	915% (?)
Increase		+12.58%	305% (?)

Here the company can issue a news release saying, truthfully, "The average gain in sales revenues of all our divisions last year was a whopping 305 percent." The analyst should be on the lookout for such language. The gain in total sales was only 12.58 percent, and that's the more meaningful number. How could Division C grow by 900 percent? Maybe it was started up in December of the year before and that year figure refers to only one full month of operation. Simple! Another rich source of intentional confusion is the use of graphs that don't show the zero point or don't display a continuous scale from zero to the values being shown. The whole subject gets complicated (see **simplicity**). In general, take all statistics with a grain of salt.

stock

Stock is the ownership account, or ownership position, in a corporation. It's a residual position, figured up by counting the assets, paying the debts, and keeping what's left over. Stock can be issued by printing certificates that provide for a certain number of shares in the ownership. The corporation will be authorized by law to issue a maximum number of shares. These shares of stock become proportional claims to all the stockholders' equity in the earnings and assets of the corporation. The stock is issued originally by the corporation in order to raise money to do business. After that, it can be traded among investors who buy and sell it, according to their own needs and foresight. In these trades, on stock *exchanges,* or **over the counter,** none of the cash that changes hands will find its way into the corporation's treasury. Individual ownership of the stock merely changes hands.

stock certificate
See **certificate: stock.**

stock dividend

Sometimes a company may wish to increase the number of shares outstanding (to lower the market price in order to give greater liquidity to the market, or for other reasons). It can do this by issuing new shares proportionally to the holders **of record.** The usual stock dividend is about 5 percent. If you hold one hundred shares, five more are issued to you. On the record date, the market price of the stock declines proportionally, so that your total market value hardly changes. The stock dividend can be used to transfer earned surplus to capital surplus—an accounting adjustment for technical purposes. Many people think stock dividends are just great. Actually they're a nuisance. They accomplish little, and they may be used to bamboozle the shareholders. Other things being equal, I'd avoid companies that habitually issue trivial driblets of stock dividends. See also **stock split.**

stock power

If your broker holds your stock registered in your name, you must endorse the stock before it can be sold. Rather than shipping the stock certificates around, the broker can send you a blank power-of-attorney form to sign, which he'll attach to your stock certificate, and which empowers him to sell and deliver your stock. It's called a stock power.

stock reinvestment plans

Some major companies offer their shareholders the option of automatic reinvestment of their cash dividends in further purchases of the company's stock. There's a slight handling fee, but it's far less than a brokerage commission. The plan permits you to acquire small amounts of stock at low transaction cost, and you have to pay taxes on the cash "constructively received" and reinvested. The plan can be beneficial in some cases. Individual analysis required.

stock split
A company can increase its shares outstanding by altering their **par value** and multiplying the number of shares. That's a stock split, and it usually involves a larger percentage increase in shares than a **stock dividend.** Two-for-one and three-for-one splits are common. As in stock dividends, lots of people think something positive has been achieved. The stock split does achieve a dramatic decline in the price per share (before the split you have 100 shares at 50; after the split, 200 shares at 25). And that may increase the volume and marketability of the shares. That's about all it does in actual fact.

stock yield
   See **yield.**

stop-loss order
See **limit order.** The "stop" order will be executed, if you're selling long, as soon as the price drops to the limit. If you're buying to cover a short, it'll be executed as soon as the price rises to the limit.

street name
Rather than have your shares registered in your own name on the corporation's books, you can have your broker hold the shares, for your account and benefit, registered in his name. This is called registering in street name. It has advantages and disadvantages. You don't have to write endorsements on certificates or stock powers in order to sell the shares, but if your broker goes bust, you may have difficulty proving (in the chaos of his bookkeeping) that you're really the owner of shares registered in his name. If you do use street name—and I do all the time—stock with the biggest and strongest brokerage firms.

striking price
The price at which an **option** (see **put** and **call**) may be exercised, the price guaranteed by the seller (writer) of the option.

strong hands
Shareholders not likely to sell soon. When a great proportion of a company's stock is held in strong hands, there's less likelihood that the price will drop suddenly in some mass dumping of shares.

suppressed inflation
   See **inflation**.

swindles
A complete history of swindles would fill the libraries of the world. Each con man invents his own technology, which becomes obsolete as soon as he introduces it. Swindling as an industry depends on a high degree of research and development, because its product is one of rapid technological obsolescence. Consequently a description of individual products is less useful than some general understanding of the methods of research. To avoid being swindled, the great law is: Keep your eye on the cash. The swindle generally involves your gaining some future claim of immense value, for which you are privileged to pay a modest sum today (in cash) to the technological innovator who is swindling you. You are told that for a small down payment, you can acquire acreage that will some day be worth many times what you have paid. You learn that a small down payment will guarantee you a position in silver or gold coins which are bound to rise in price, but you aren't told that your contract is backed, perhaps, by nothing more than a futures contract. You are invited to send cash now for an exclusive product that exists, at the

moment, far over the seas. In all these cases, watch where the cash goes. Find out the names of the people who are to perform the guarantees in the contract you buy, and see if they're reputable, if they have the financial resources to back up a long-term contract, and if they've indeed already performed the services they claim to have performed. Beware the hustle. If someone tells you this offer expires in fifteen minutes, ask yourself why. See **haste** and **simplicity.** Ask for physical verification of the goods; ask for business references. Remember: the two principal emotions that the swindler will play on are your greed and your fear. If you find a smooth-talking gentleman building up your fear or your greed—or both—be on your guard. Ask for time to think it over. Ask him to call you back in a couple of weeks. By then he'll be in the next town, and *you'll* have your cash.

Swiss this & that
Magic word, Switzerland. Alps, fortress. Banks, rich. Accounts, secret. People, solid. All this, plus yodeling and cuckoo clocks and chocolate bonbons!

banks
Yes, you can have a secret account in a Swiss bank. However, if the Swiss authorities suspect you of having violated *their* law, they have the power to invade the privacy of your account. From time to time, when the flow of money gets out of hand, the Swiss slap a penalty tax on any new deposits. Watch out for that. And they charge a good price for handling your account; after all, the secrecy involves additional administrative labor. If you rely on the Swiss banks for investment advice, you should expect merely average performance. Swiss money managers tend to look three centuries into the future and be satisfied with earning the market rate of interest on investment funds. Perhaps the best-kept secret in Swiss banking is the lousy investment results of Swiss-managed portfolios.

francs

The Swiss franc used to be considered sound, i.e., impervious to inflation. It has been inflated at rates of 10 percent or so in recent years and has, from time to time, suffered even worse than the dollar. Nevertheless, the Swiss franc will probably maintain its buying power slightly better than the dollar; perhaps in the next ten years the dollar will lose 60 or 70 percent of today's buying power while the Swiss franc will lose only 30 percent. That's small consolation. Better to escape the paper fiat stuff of all countries and move into gold or silver. If it's geographical diversification that attracts you to Switzerland, just have the Swiss bank store some gold and silver bullion for you. Expect a storage fee of 1 or 2 percent a year.

investments

Swiss companies are known around the world. Swissair, Nestlé, Ciba, Swiss Bank Corporation. A large portfolio might hold a few such stocks in the interest of geographical diversification. Their investment performance, however, will be in line with the development of the world economy, and not much better. Any large American international company would do the same for you, and spare you the problems of international finance. Try to buy them at times when there's no penalty on new capital inflows.

T

taking profits

"You never go broke taking profits," says the old wisdom, but it's directly contradictory to the more fundamental wisdom of letting your profits run (see **let your profits run**). True, it's easier to buy a stock at the right price than to sell it at the right price. The problem arises because you have two problems in selling. You have to find a good high price for the sale—perhaps somewhere near the top—and then you have to reinvest the proceeds in something that will do better than what you sold. Taking profits just for the sake of taking profits is foolish. In general, before you give the order to sell, make sure you have a definite plan for the reinvestment of the proceeds. If you look around and find nothing attractive in the stock market, think twice; this may be a signal that the whole structure of stock prices is unrealistically high, and instead of selling and reinvesting you should be selling everything and going into sheltered positions until prices look more normal.

tangible goods

After an inflation has proceeded long enough to persuade everyone that the money is steadily growing worthless, people develop a general and pervasive desire to trade in their money for almost anything else available in the markets. This is called a **flight from money** or a "flight into tangible goods." It's a tricky time for investors, because there's a widespread belief that you can make profits in anything whose price goes up (see **interest: real**). When the value of the money is changing so fast, it becomes difficult to distinguish an apparent profit from a real one. At this point in an inflation, the best tangible goods are those that are basic to life. Lay in the supply of food, clothing, fuel—things you can consume in your ordinary rounds of life. Since they have an unvarying value in relation to your own needs, you can ignore their price in the wild inflationary markets. The thing to avoid is mere haphazard accumulation of things you can't use—a hundred broomsticks, a thousand pounds of salt, and so on.

tape
The tickertape that reports stock transactions from the floor of the stock exchange. "Don't argue with the tape." See also **anticipation.**

tax-exempt bond
See **bond: municipal.**

tax shelter
An investment device that permits you to deduct from taxable income an amount greater than your cash outlay for the investment. Typical fields are oil, cattle, real estate, mining, and film production.

technical analysis
See **security analysis** and **random walk.**

third market
Not a listed exchange. Not OTC. Direct trading among principals and investors of blocks of stock.

timing
Don't try to cut things too fine. If you want to buy or sell, do it at the market (see **market: at the market**). There are occasions when you can use a **limit order** (an order to execute a transaction only if the stock hits a certain

preselected price), but you can safely ignore such technicalities all your life and still manage a handsome portfolio program. Looking for the top tick or the bottom tick has kept many an investor from enjoying a good long ride. This reminds me that there are three reasons often given for refusing to buy a stock: 1) it has been going down, 2) it hasn't been going anywhere, and 3) it has risen recently. These are reasons given by tick-watchers who have lost sight of the long-term forces at work.

topping out
See **bottoming out,** and turn it upside down.

total investment yield
Same as overall investment yield (see **overall return**): cash return plus change in capital values or market values.

total portfolio yield
Same as above.

touting
Touting is any unremitting effort to sell something. Some brokers get in the habit of loading up their clients with a given stock. A few people touting the same stock can run the price up and make everyone look good for a short time. Don't buy anything unless *you* think the underlying fundamentals are attractive and the price is reasonable. The tout will tell you, "You better buy it today! The price is going to rise!" You can reply that in this business all the big mistakes are made in a hurry, and would he please send you some further information about the company.

trading
See **gambling.** No offense intended.

tranquility
One of the necessary conditions of a successful investment program. See **personal factors.** If your portfolio keeps you awake at night, even though in strict financial terms it's the perfect one for you, it's not doing you any good as a person. Shelter it until you feel secure. That's the maximum effectiveness you should strive for.

transaction date
Date on which your trade is executed.

transfer agent
If a company doesn't keep it's own record of who owns the shares issued, it hires a bank to serve as transfer agent. The bank keeps track of the name and address of the owner of each stock certificate—quite a chore when you consider that fifteen or twenty million shares change hands (and names) each day on the New York Stock Exchange alone.

transportation
A basic industry, but one unfortunately regulated to the point of suffocation by the federal government. See also **industrials.**

air freight
The fastest growing and most promising sector of the whole industry. Revenue growth is well above 10 percent a year. Some contracyclical tendencies: when the economy at large is bad, shippers send a larger quantity of smaller packages to make up for businessmen's decisions to carry less in stock.

airlines

Cyclical, overregulated, poorly managed, overequipped, overpriced. If granted the freedom to compete by lowering their fares, the airlines could be a magnificent industry, and the traveler would get cheaper transportation. But the government doesn't see it that way.

railroads

If the rails could get rid of outmoded labor rules (as Florida East Coast has), they'd cut their expense ratio by half, have plenty to spend on improved equipment and service, and still show a handsome profit. But the unions—with federal approval—don't see it that way. The consequence is that the rails may some day be nationalized, adding about $5 billion of their deficits to the budget the taxpayers have to meet. Some regional rails (Southern Railway) and some special situations (the Pocahontas rails) may hold out longer than the rest.

shipping

Forget it. Maritime unions are in cahoots with the politicians, shipping companies have their hands in the subsidy trough, and everyone is hiding behind the protection of privileged laws and rulings. America's merchant marine used to be the best in the world. But that was in the nineteenth century, before Washington decided to manage it for the benefit of the favored few.

trucking

If you like the combination of federal regulation and the Teamsters Union, here's your cup of tea. Trucking routes are protected monopolies and can be profitable; but their existence depends on political connections, and that's not the soundest ground for a long-term investment.

tree

"The tree does not grow to the sky"; i.e., don't be greedy. Don't expect every **bubble** to go on forever. Be prepared to sell before the market stops rising. A difficult thing to do, and contradictory to the idea of holding on for the long term. But if you can accurately identify the bubble, you can change the rules.

trend

A trend is any tendency to move in one direction. Trends can last a long time or a short time. Short trends may be no longer than a season or a year: *seasonal* trends. They may last through a business cycle and eventually be seen to have been fluctuating around a central point, rather than moving in one direction: *cyclical* trends. They may be genuine long-term movements in one direction: *secular* trends. See also **cycles.** Note the slight hint of fashionableness or faddishness in the idea of a trend. True in finance too.

trusts

In general, avoid them. If you can't avoid them, see if you can retain control of the investment policy guiding the trust. If you're the beneficiary and the banker has sole authority, seduce the banker.

turnabout, turnaround

A turnaround situation exists when the company that has fallen on bad times suddenly acquires the ability to improve its fortunes. The stock will have fallen to low levels and staggered along, perhaps for years. No one is interested. You can buy all the stock you want at giveaway prices. You do. And sooner or later the ugly duckling turns into the fairy princess. Congratulations!

U

underwriter
See **investment banker.**

union labor
Not a bad thing in itself. *Monopoly* practices, condoned by the government, are what get in the way of progress.

unit of trading
In stock, usually one hundred shares. See **round lot.** In bonds, five or ten $1,000 bonds. In commodities, contracts worth $5,000 or $10,000 at a whack.

utilities
All of them are regulated by government. State commissions vary in their understanding of the relation between capital investment and productive efficiency. Most commissions see the investor as the enemy and the "public" as the voter-friend. Hence the poor performance of utilities under inflationary conditions.

electric
Underperformers. However, the long-term outlook for a few, here and there, where population growth is fast and where the rate commissions aren't entirely Maoist, is perhaps better than average. Florida; Texas; that's about it.

gas
Forget it. The bureaucrats will never let you earn a dime.

telephone

Slow death. But if the phone companies were ever permitted to compete with the Post Office, there'd be fine things on the horizon.

water

Local, slow, so-so. Prosit!

V

variable annuity
See **insurance: annuity,** but remember that a variable annuity is only as good as the common stock investment program behind it. Why *pay* an institution merely to do an institutional job for you, when you can probably handle your own investments with better results and lower cost?

venture capital
A *venture* is any business opportunity which may promise a large profit, but is undertaken with the knowledge that it entails a high degree of risk. An oil drilling program, a movie production budget, a new research effort, the launching of a new kind of business—all these are straight ventures. The capital raised for them is venture capital, and there are firms that specialize in raising and investing this kind of capital. Usually venture capital is scraped together from the speculative sectors of large investors' portfolios. The rate of success is extremely low on new ventures, something like 5 percent. So, rich or poor, the average investor should not expose more than 5 percent of his total portfolio to capital ventures. Well-managed venture capital firms think they're lucky to make 30 percent on the total funds they manage.

volume
Volume of trading is the number of shares traded in a given period of time. Low volume of trading means low liquidity and poor marketability of the stock. It's best to avoid stepping into the market when volume is running far above

or far below normal. Volume enters into many systems of technical analysis, none of which work. See **random walk.** Excessively high volume can be a sign of churning. In that case, stand back and wait until you can find out which way the ball will bounce.

W

Wall Street vs. Main Street

Wall Street is the old financial center of New York, rich in the history of bombs, scandals, and crashes, rich also in the mythology of its ability to victimize the innocent lad from Main Street, U.S.A. There's more than a grain of truth behind every myth. The thoroughly naïve should not go about Wall Street unchaperoned. But it is also true that Wall Street raises the billions of dollars of capital that builds factories and schools, and that no naïve lad can be injured until he has permitted his greed to be inflamed. Use good judgment. If someone promises you the moon, use doubly good judgment. See also **swindles.**

wallpaper

Worthless stock certificates.

warrant

An **option,** issued by a company, authorizing the holder to buy shares of common stock at a guaranteed price. Some warrants are perpetual (until exercised, of course). Others have expiration dates. They can be spectacular speculative vehicles. But they pay no income, and they may fall flat. So, if you must play with them, go easy.

wash transactions

A wash transaction occurs when you buy something through one channel and sell it simultaneously through another, with no real effect on your cash or your holdings. Such transactions may be engineered for tax purposes, or in order to give the illusion of large-volume trading in a stock. Tax laws strictly govern wash sales, while any subterfuge to create the illusion of activity is frowned on by the SEC. The rules apply to identical or substantially identical securities. They do not apply to simultaneous purchase and sale of different securities, even though their market actions may be related. You can, for example, buy a silver futures contract due in a given month and sell one for the next month. The two contracts are different securities. Since they tend to have similar market actions, you get the effect of a wash transaction. Since you are both long and short the same commodity, one of your contracts will show a gain and one will show a loss, whether the price goes up or down. You can then simply select which one you want to sell for tax purposes. If you have capital gains which you wish to shelter, sell the contract with a loss, offsetting the gains and reducing the tax bill. Hold on to the contract with a gain and throw that sale into the next tax year. Nice game!

wave theory

This theory of market behavior says there are three types of waves or **cycles** in stock prices: 1) the day-to-day fluctuations, 2) the medium-term ups and downs, and 3) the great years-long bear and bull markets. Much is made of the conjunctions and disjunctions of the three, and of the effect of sunspots (which do correlate with great market rises and falls). But (see **random walk**) there really isn't any pattern in day-to-day price changes, and the medium-term price change depends on the choice of time period, which choice is mostly arbitrary. So we are left with the idea that the market has great long rising spells and great long sinking spells. Which is what we knew before we started, plus the sunspots. Call it baloney, and move on.

{#}

weak hands

See also **strong hands.** The weak ones are the short-time Charlies who are in for a quick ride and will dump the stock as soon as it stops doubling every five minutes. Weak hands are the investor's name for the speculator. Strong hands are the speculator's name for the investor.

wealth

Whatever provides satisfactions. Basically, things. By extension, the money flow that permits you to buy things. By further extension, the capital that permits you to claim the money flow. By final extension, the paper certificates that give evidence of your ownership of the capital. But these last are the more abstract and theoretical forms of wealth. Never forget the wealth is whatever provides satisfactions, and that includes whatever gives you sound sleep, time off, good company, and a serene heart.

when issued

Stock payable on record date, as a result of a new issue. A **stock dividend,** or a **stock split,** can be traded from hand to hand, even though the certificates haven't been printed and registered as yet. This is stock trading on a when-issued basis. You'll see it quoted in the papers as "w.i."

whipsaw

Saddest of events for the trader, the whipsaw occurs when he does everything wrong. He buys at 30. The stock goes to 25 and he sells, taking his loss quickly as a professional should. For some reason he averts his gaze and the next thing he knows the stock is selling at 35. He wades in and sells short, thinking the stock will drop. It goes to 40. He buys to cover and once again takes a loss. The stock drops to 30. He buys long. It drops to 25 . . . and so on. When this begins to happen, it's best to acknowledge defeat. It's a stock you don't understand, and one or two sour trades should convince you that you're on alien ground. For trading purposes, try to find five or six stocks you think you understand, and spend your time playing with them.

windfalls

Suppose you inherit twenty thousand dollars, or win fifty thousand dollars in the lottery, or simply rob a bank. How should you invest this windfall sum? First, don't be in a hurry. You got along fine without an investment portfolio all these years. You can live another month while you hold the cash and think about your plans. Select an investment adviser, if need be. Shoot for a well diversified portfolio (see **diversification**). Don't buy everything at once, but plan to put the money to work in three or four pieces, with a month or two between buying points. If prices don't act as you expected, change your buying plans. You will, of course, have to decide whether you should pay off the mortgage, invest in education, take a trip, buy raw land, invest in coins, and so on. Each of these alternatives is discussed separately in this book. Indeed, the whole book is the answer to the question of handling a windfall. You should be so lucky!

wire house

A brokerage house with lots of branch offices in distant cities, wiring their orders to the main office.

working capital

Net current assets. The difference between current assets and current liabilities.

write-off

Any deduction, especially one taken for tax purposes, is a write-off. The cost of equipment can be written off, through bookkeeping entries, as a charge against taxable income (see **depreciation**). It is possible to get a write-off that exceeds the amount of your cash expenditure (see **tax shelter**).

writing options

Selling other people the right to buy your stock at a guaranteed price for a stated period of time. You gain cash income when you sell the option. Only a fraction of such options are ever exercised, so the cash from the sale of the option is an enhancement of the cash yield of the portfolio. Sometimes, by writing options, you can guarantee yourself 15 or 20 percent on your money, on a yearly basis. That's well worth shooting for! But it's also a short-term solution to the perennial problem of investment, and perhaps over a number of years it wouldn't be as profitable as a well-managed portfolio of growth stocks. It's worth knowing about, however. And if it turns out you have a knack for it, keep it up!

X

X-ray
You should develop X-ray vision in reading financial statements—indeed, in reading the daily press. Much of the story is between the lines or in the fine print of the footnotes. Take nothing at face value. See also **hidden problems, hidden values, balance sheet, earnings.**

Y

yield
Yield is the investment return; the cash income from an investment; the interest or dividend income. It's usually figured as a percentage, and there are various different bases on which to make the calculation. See also **bond yield.**

direct
Direct yield is the ratio between cash income and the cash cost of the investment.

to maturity
Yield to maturity includes cash income and whatever change in market value there may be between the price paid for the bond and the par value or redemption value of the bond (stocks don't have maturity dates). Yield to maturity includes an accrued income, if the bond is bought at a discount; an accrued cost, if it's bought at a premium.

overall
See **overall return.** In relation to stocks, the overall return is the cash income plus the change in market values. Some people also figure the profits retained in the business as part of the broadly conceived investment return on the stock. See also **earnings.**

Z

zero growth

Ecological enthusiasts argue that there are too many people, and that we should set our goal at zero population growth. This does not automatically mean zero economic growth, because economic growth is the result of increased productivity per capita. Faced with the prospect of continued economic growth with a stabilized population, some zero-growth people will assail the objective of economic growth on the grounds that further progress means further pollution, and so on. The same people deplore the existence of the poor, the aged, the ill, and express compassion for them. But if there is to be no increase in the stream of wealth nor in the population, while there *is* to be an increase in the flow of wealth toward some groups, there must be a forcible redirection of the income stream, in accord with the orders and directives of the ecologists. It would seem that the ultimate result of zero-growth theories would be some form of dictated economy. It is worth observing that zero-growth enthusiasts exist only in free-market countries. In the dictated economies, growth is not a problem. It's a dream.

Appendix A

Here are some useful sources of current information on financial and business matters.

Newspapers

Finanz and Wirtschaft—printed in Zurich, Switzerland; written in German; good source of financial data on European markets, prices, and companies

London Financial Times—from London, England; major source of worldwide financial and market news

Northern Miner—from Toronto, Canada; authoritative if slightly breathless reports on mining activities in Canada and elsewhere

South African Financial Gazette—from Johannesburg, South Africa; thorough review of South African business and economics; strong reporting on the gold- and diamond-mining industries; general coverage only as it applies to investment situation

Via Française—from Paris, France; written in French; great statistical coverage of French markets and securities; numerous analyses of companies and issues in each issue; good coverage of gold, silver, and monetary trends; stock recommendations not to be relied upon

Wall Street Journal—edited in New York, with regional editions from Chicago, Dallas, West Coast; magnificent financial and economic coverage; also highly regarded as cultural commentator, with frequent articles of general interest, based on expert reporting and writing; news summaries in twin columns on front page are the best in the business

Newsletters

Financial Book Digest—reviews of 80–100 investment books
per year, including how-to books on general family
finance; objective; favorable reviews to one book out of
ten; *Library Journal* says: "Reviews are brash and pull
no punches . . . . Aimed at the intelligent, do-it-yourself
investor, this is enjoyable reading even if you never
buy a book—and very useful to the public library
selecting books for good circulation potential but
wanting to avoid trash"

First National City Bank Monthly Letter—from the Bank,
in New York City; well written but semi-official and so
fangless and clawless; discussion of current trends in
business, finance, economics, international affairs only
tangentially useful to the investor

Morgan Guaranty Survey—from the Bank, in New York
City; verbose, dilute, but "authoritative" and so in-
dicative of what may be coming

Magazines

Barron's—from Dow Jones, in New York City; most complete statistical tables of securities prices, market
indices, financial and economic indicators; occasional
articles with useful material for investment decisions

Business Week—from McGraw-Hill, New York City; a
useful roundup of business news

International Background—from Vaduz, Liechtenstein;
written in English by foreigners; authoritative, analytical, objective, original discussions of current trends in
politics and business all over the world; editor is a
resolute technical analyst of stock markets but has
been successful

Mining Journal—from London, England; basic journal for
the world mining industry

Annual Reports
Available on request from any company you ask

Investment Services
Moody's—New York; complete services
Rickenbacker Report—Briarcliff Manor, New York; newsletter and portfolio management
Standard & Poor—New York; complete services

Research Organizations
American Institute for Economic Research—Great Barrington, Massachusetts; periodic reports, analyses; portfolio counseling available
Federal Reserve Bank of St. Louis—St. Louis, Missouri; numerous publications, mainly analyzing monetary trends and their effects on other economic series; highly useful to those who put emphasis on monetary events
Federal Reserve Board—Washington, D.C.; many different publications, covering money, banking, economic statistics; thoroughly academic, official, pallid, but authoritative and cheap
Department of Commerce—Washington, D.C.; many publications on business and economic matters; Bureau of Labor Statistics is the big number-grinder; but the numbers are issued with varying lags; don't count on them for predictive features

Appendix B

Here's a listing of the most useful books published in recent years—books useful to the person who has just begun to take a serious interest in financial planning. The books cover the basic ground of investment selection and money management; basic theory of economics and investment; and the history of great swindles and frauds—just to remind you that this can be serious business! The reviews are from the *Financial Book Digest,* and are published here in condensed form with the consent of the publisher of FBD, William F. Rickenbacker. The reviews were written variously by myself and the editor of FBD, Mr. Timothy J. Wheeler.

The Battle for Stock Market Profits
Gerald M. Loeb
New York: Simon & Schuster, 1971.
There is much practical wisdom on the selection of stocks, the evaluation of investment information, the usefulness of mutual funds and investment advisers and go-go operators.

Loeb's earlier book, *The Battle for Investment Survival,* is to be preferred. But this one is easy reading and harmless hobnobbing with riches. Recommended for the beginner, and also for the investor who has never been able to make his portfolio grow and stay out of trouble.

Money and Markets: A Monetarist View
Beryl W. Sprinkel
Homewood, Illinois: Dow Jones–Irwin, 1971.
Every so often, a book appears that is destined to reach

beyond the conventional approaches, to lay the theoretical foundations for a revolutionary new technique in predicting market movements.

Dr. Sprinkel grounded his case in the "Chicago school" monetarist economics of Milton Friedman. His thesis, very simply, is that the amount of money in circulation is an important—perhaps the most important—determinant of economic activity in general and the stock market in particular.

One day monetary data will play as large a role on the Wall Street scene as the hourly Dow Jones averages do today. Until then, this book offers not only a potent tool for timing investments, but a decided advantage over the many who haven't learned its secrets.

"Do You Sincerely Want to Be Rich?": The Full Story of Bernard Cornfeld and IOS
Charles Raw, Bruce Page, and Godfrey Hodgson
New York: The Viking Press, 1971.

Three British journalists spent a year putting together all the patches in Bernard Cornfeld's crazy-quilt financial empire. This book, the result of an amazing amount of detective work, is probably the closest we shall come to understanding just what happened in Investors Overseas Services.

Careful study of this prize of financial journalism is recommended to every investor who thinks the world is honest, and every investor who thinks he is beyond the reach of greed and folly.

The Funny Money Game
Andrew Tobias
Chicago: Playboy Press, 1971.

Altogether too much of the book is devoted by Mr. Tobias to Mr. Tobias, a rather empty-headed young man of twenty-four with pedigree, Harvard education, and deferred radical ambitions (he prudently allotted three to five years to make his million before going out to save the world). The story he tells about The National Student Marketing Corporation differs only in detail from those of other funny money conglomerates, of IOS, of go-go funds and high-fliers, of chain letters and the Ponzi game and the Department of Health, Education, and Welfare, and any other chic swindle you can name. It is the depressing but instructive story of greed, highly contagious greed. We learn again that greed overcomes our sense, makes us into fools and liars, and finally smashes us down, empty-handed. (The author thinks "the system" is to blame.)

There are a a few bonus insights about 21-year-old vice presidents of $100 million corporate empires, if you can take it. The book has no value for investment advice, but you may want to read it as a study in human nature.

The Intelligent Investor
Benjamin Graham
New York: Harper & Row, 1965.
Here, for our money, is as good a market manual as your money can buy. We don't risk much with the opinion: *The Intelligent Investor* has been in print since 1949. Its guidelines have been tested and retested, not only in all the standard phases of the market cycle but also in the unprecedented bull market following World War II. Dow Theory ceased to be useful in that prolonged rise, because the Dow flashed "buy" signals at higher levels than its previous "sell" signals. The investor taking Graham's advice would have been able to ride out fluctuations for a far larger profit.

If you already own a copy of the book, make it a point to read it every year or two. If you don't have one, buy one. A library copy isn't enough: you'll want one you can reach for in the crisis, study at leisure, and fill with dogeared pages and underlined passages.

Unaccountable Accounting
Abraham J. Briloff
New York: Harper & Row, 1972.

Briloff goes through the basic lessons of accounting and then takes you along as he tracks down the distortions and concealments in the financial statements of notorious shyster operations. He names names: Leasco, Litton, IOS, National General, National Student Marketing, Telex, Memorex, Lockheed, Great Southwest, Penn Central, Occidental Petroleum, Bernie Cornfeld, John King, and more. He writes with great energy and color, and he's as fearless as that young insurance specialist, Dirks, who blew the whistle on Equity Funding. The book is good reading for anyone interested in accountancy. For the serious investor who does a lot of his own research and who knows how to take financial statements apart and put them back together again, the book is a gold mine of new techniques for spotting foul play.

Uncommon Profits Through Stock Purchase Warrants
S. L. Prendergast
Homewood, Illinois: Dow Jones–Irwin, 1973.

Here is everything you need to know about warrants, by far the best study we've ever seen on the subject. It is a pity the subject itself is so restricted. But, for those who are interested in warrants, here is holy writ.

The Dow Theory Can Make You Rich
Robert M. Barnes
New Rochelle: Arlington, 1973.

The author describes six main investment techniques that employ "Dow Theory." (The Dow Theory says that stocks have long-term moves upward and downward, and within those swings they have shorter moves in the opposite direction.) After a great deal of shop talk, the author evaluates the six techniques over a period of years.

Frauds, Swindles, and Rackets
Robert S. Rosefsky
Chicago: Follett, 1973.

Mr. Rosefsky is a swindle hunter. Writer of a syndicated column on money management, he encounters all sorts of con games, and has catalogued a vast array of them in this fascinating book. He shows how swindlers play on the victim's greed. He tells you how to recognize and avoid a swindle, and even how to get help. This isn't an investment book per se, but its lessons apply, for greed is equally ruinous in the market. Knowledge of fraudulent practices and a nose for skulduggery are indispensable to the defensive investor.

A Random Walk Down Wall Street
Burton G. Malkiel
New York: Norton, 1973.

In readability and usefulness, this is the best guidebook to personal investment thinking since Benjamin Graham's *The Intelligent Investor.*

Malkiel tops off his book with an excellent program for individual investment, and there is nothing "random" about the way he advises you to manage your money. He does mention certain unproven assumptions in the random-walk theory and he does hold out the possibility of superior investment results based on superior fundamental analysis. He is, finally, a moderate man, believing that intelligence and prudence will do better than random selection.

All in all, a fine and sensible book. Every investor, from beginner to professional, can learn something from it.

The Long and the Short of Hedging
Jarrott T. Miller
Chicago: Regnery, 1973.
This is a rock-solid instruction book that concentrates on
the use of warrants and their related common stocks for the
purpose of setting up hedged positions. There is a succinct
and accurate glossary as well as a helpful index. If you have
an interest in warrants, hedging, straddles, puts, calls,
convertibles—you can use this book to advantage.

The Failure of the "New Economics"
Henry Hazlitt
New Rochelle: Arlington, 1973.
Keynes's *General Theory of Employment, Interest, and
Money* was published in 1936. The *General Theory* is still
doing a thriving business all over the world, its popularity
today, as from the beginning, is based on its reputation as
the theoretical refutation of classical and free market
economics. In 1959 Mr. Henry Hazlitt analyzed the *General
Theory* chapter by chapter, line by line, and revealed it to
be a showpiece of confusion, and utterly wrong in its attack
on free markets. It is good to have this overwhelming
refutation of Keynesianism available again.

How to Buy Foreign Securities
Rainer Esslen
Frenchtown, New Jersey: Columbia Publishing, 1974.
The author advises that the safest entry into the field is with
foreign securities traded actively in the U.S., domestic
corporations with substantial earnings abroad, or American
Depositary Receipts. Beyond these one gets into deep
water. The book includes a glossary and a series of graphs
comparing capital investment and growth in various countries with a weighted "world index"—in effect, thumbnail

sketches of a given country's investment performance (1959–1973), and possible indicators of things to come. A fine job. . . .

The Figure Finaglers
Robert Reichard
New York: McGraw-Hill, 1974.
This is the age of statistics, and everyone should, in self-defense, learn a bit about how charts and figures can be used to deceive. Mr. Reichard's book is a satisfactory introduction to statistical distortions, and no great facility with mathematics is required to understand it.

Conservative Investors Sleep Well
Philip A. Fisher
New York: Harper & Row, 1975.
Mr. Fisher's idea of a conservative investment is not necessarily the established blue-chip firm with a good dividend history, as you might suppose. What he looks for is a company that is superbly managed, flexible, and future-oriented, the most competitive in its field, part of an essential industry, and undervalued by the investment community. . . . The author recommends massive research going far beyond deskwork before buying. He stresses fundamentals, including such qualities as conservative accounting and good personnel management. . . . This book has a rare blend of sophistication and guidance for the investor.